Learning
for
Life

This book is proudly and affectionately dedicated to the memory of R. C. Bradley, an extraordinary man—husband, father, mentor, and passionate believer in the dignity of all people, particularly young children. His influence in the lives of thousands of learners is a legacy that will endure.

Ronald J. Areglado
Pamela S. Lane

Learning for Life

Creating Classrooms for Self-Directed Learning

Ronald J. Areglado
R. C. Bradley
Pamela S. Lane

CORWIN PRESS, INC.
A Sage Publications Company
Thousand Oaks, California

For information address:

CORWIN
PRESS

Corwin Press, Inc.
2455 Teller Road
Thousand Oaks, California 91320
E-mail: order@sagepub.com

SAGE Publications Ltd.
6 Bonhill Street
London EC2A 4PU
United Kingdom

SAGE Publications India Pvt. Ltd.
M-32 Market
Greater Kailash I
New Delhi 110 048 India

Printed in the United States of America

Library of Congress Cataloging-in-Publication Data

Areglado, Ronald J.
    Learning for life: creating classrooms for self-directed learning /
authors, Ronald J. Areglado, R. C. Bradley, Pamela S. Lane.
        p. cm.
    Includes bibliographical references and index.
    ISBN 0-8039-6385-8 (cloth: acid-free paper).—ISBN 0-8039-6386-6
(pbk.: acid-free paper)
    1. Individualized instruction—United States   2. Learning
Psychology of.   3. Classroom management—United States.   4. School
management and organization—United States.   5. Self-culture—United
States.   I. Bradley, R. C.   II. Lane, Pamela S.   III. Title.
LB1031.A44   1996
371.3'94—dc20   96-4476

This book is printed on acid-free paper.

96 97 98 99 00 10 9 8 7 6 5 4 3 2 1

Corwin Press Production Editor: Vicki Baker
Corwin Press Typesetter: Marion S. Warren

Contents

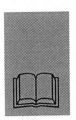

Foreword

*L*earning for Life, by Areglado, Bradley, and Lane, may well be one of the most important books ever written on the subject of self-directed learning (SDL). It offers an innovative program for significantly improving learning and teaching, and for attaining excellence in education.

In this age when sudden, unexpected change is becoming the norm, we search constantly for educational tools that can help people learn how to adjust to the changes in their lives, to acquire knowledge and skills to cope with such changes, and to fully develop their human potential and creative talents. This book is such a tool. Well written and organized, it provides the reader with a wealth of ideas, information, concepts, and methods of self-directed learning. The authors, all top educators with extensive teaching experience, have amply documented and illustrated the self-directed learning methodology with practical examples.

Areglado, Bradley, and Lane conceptualize SDL as a synergistic process, in which a teacher helps learners use various strategies and perceptual skills to learn on their own, become more responsible for their learning, and get in charge of their own lives.

SDL enables learners not only to acquire knowledge of subject matter, but also to understand themselves and their work habits, perceptions, aspirations, value systems, and potential. It helps students rely on their own learning power instead of depending solely on the teacher. It also teaches them how to work cooperatively with others, treating them with respect and dignity.

Self-directed learning helps students to become motivated, to have a better understanding of themselves and others, and to be able to take control of their own lives and destinies. SDL shapes the learners' behavior, leading them to become responsible, honest, caring people.

Dr. George E. Lasker
President and Chairman of the Board
International Institute for Advanced Studies
in Systems Research and Cybernetics
University of Windsor
Windsor, Ontario, Canada

Acknowledgments

During the completion of this book, our coauthor and dear friend R. C. Bradley passed away. We wish to acknowledge R. C.'s wife, Marilyn, whose indomitable positive spirit and inspiration enabled us to finish our work.

We want to extend our deepest appreciation to our families for their unwavering support and encouragement.

Special thanks to Mrs. Sue Doyle, our computer processor and expert, who followed this manuscript from beginning to end; to John Dawson, who field-tested several of our ideas; and to Todd Hoffman and Ken Thomas, who made significant contributions to several of the chapters.

Likewise, we wish to thank Constance Austin, Carmen Crowsley, Paul Jennings, Barbara McPherson, Henry Peel, Maria Shelton, William Uhrik, and Jean Williamson for providing us with background information, research, and classroom scenarios detailing their use of self-directed learning.

We are also indebted to Gracia Alkema, President, and Alice Foster, Acquisitions Editor, of Corwin Press, for their belief in the usefulness of the ideas in our book, and to Louanne Wheeler, Assistant Director of Publications for NAESP, whose indispen-

sable and exceptional editing skills brought vitality and clarity to
our work.

Finally, we thank the children, teachers, and administrators
of our nation's schools, who comprise a powerful community of
self-directed learners.

About the Authors

Dr. Ronald J. Areglado is the Associate Executive Director of Programs for the National Association of Elementary School Principals (NAESP), Alexandria, Virginia, which serves more than 26,000 elementary and middle school principals throughout the United States and overseas. He received his B.S. from Boston State College (1967), his M.Ed. from Boston University (1971), and his Ed.D. from the University of Massachusetts, Amherst (1982).

Dr. Areglado has held a variety of positions in the education field. He was a teacher in the Boston Public Schools, a rural elementary school principal and superintendent in western Massachusetts, and an official for the Commonwealth of Massachusetts Department of Education. In addition, he has been an adjunct professor at several New England colleges and universities, teaching courses in educational leadership.

Throughout his career, Dr. Areglado has consulted with both for-profit and non-profit groups on a range of organizational behavior and leadership issues. He has conducted numerous workshops throughout the country on the role of the principal, and has been a keynote speaker and panelist for conferences, symposia, and national radio and television talk shows.

Dr. Areglado is a recipient of several professional and community awards. He was chosen by *Executive Educator* magazine as one of North America's "Top 100 School Executives" in 1980.

Dr. R. C. Bradley was Professor of Education at the University of North Texas, in Denton, for 32 years. He received his Educational Specialist degree from Central Missouri State University in 1962, and his Ed.D. from the University of Missouri at Columbia in 1963. Each institution granted him their Distinguished Alumni Award for his contributions to education and society.

Dr. Bradley spoke nationally and internationally to a variety of audiences, associations (including ASCD and NAESP), and school districts across the United States, Canada, Mexico, and Germany. He served as a teacher, supervisor, administrator, and college professor. He spent 17 years as Editor-in-Chief of the *TEPSA Journal,* served on the editorial board of *Contemporary Education Journal,* and on writing and editing teams for several national groups. He held memberships in numerous professional organizations, including the International Institute for Advanced Studies in Systems Research and Cybernetics. He authored more than 200 articles for professional journals, as well as monographs and book chapters. *Helping Students Become Self-Directed Learners* was his 19th book.

Dr. Bradley believed that by becoming more self-directed, you can make a difference in the lives of others.

Dr. Pamela S. Lane is a fifth-grade teacher at Eva Swan Hodge Elementary School in Denton, Texas. She received her Ed.D. from the University of North Texas, in Denton, in 1992.

Dr. Lane's pioneering study, "A Quasi-Experimental Study of Fifth Graders' Use of Self-Directing Perceptions and Learning Strategies," focused on two major areas of self-directedness: the perceptual—students controlling their own thinking processes for improved behavior and learning strategies; and higher-level skills—including metacognitive map-making, automatization of all acquired skills, and cybernetic theory applied to perceptions.

She has been involved in education as a teacher, college professor, and supervisor. During 1993-1994, she served as professional development site coordinator for the Early Childhood Professional Site at Hodge Elementary School in Denton.

Dr. Lane's professional workshops include topics such as Professional Development Programs, Facilitating Play in the Early Childhood Setting, and Discipline in the Self-Directing Classroom. In 1994, her dissertation was nominated for Phi Delta Kappa's Outstanding Dissertation Award.

CORWIN
PRESS

The Corwin Press logo—a raven striding across an open book—represents the happy union of courage and learning. We are a professional-level publisher of books and journals for K-12 educators, and we are committed to creating and providing resources that embody these qualities. Corwin's motto is "Success for All Learners."

What Is Self-Directed Learning?

*In the school of the future, students will learn to educate them-
selves, focusing attention not only on acquiring subject matter
but on understanding their own work habits, knowledge bases,
insights, aspirations, value systems, how they learn best, and
personal talents. This fundamental change—self-directing one's
own learning instead of depending solely on a teacher—is the
biggest challenge that education will face.*

In recent years, technological advances and a changing society
have ushered us into a strange new world in which rapid change
seems to be the only stable characteristic (Knowles, 1975). We
have made no real moves to change our educational system to fit
the pace of change, and our stimulus-response environment in
school does not do a lot to keep learners turned on to learning
(Rogers, 1969). As computers began to take over some of the basics
in education, schools began to consider new roles—teaching values, ethics, motivation, and more.

We now realize that with knowledge doubling every 6 months, there is no way that schools can continue only as transmitters of knowledge. Former President Bush acknowledged the need for a change in school focus, saying, "Education is not just about making a living; it is also about making a life" (*America 2000, 1991*). He urged every American to continue learning throughout life, using the myriad formal and informal means available to gain further knowledge and skills—a call for self-direction of the highest order!

When a person leaves school today, he or she must not only have a foundation of knowledge but, more important, also the skills of a self-directed learner, prepared to keep on acquiring knowledge. Schools of the future must focus on developing skills for inquiry, reasoning, memory, creativity, interpersonal relations, metacognition, and perceptual control. Self-directed learners will thus have a powerful hold on learning for the rest of their lives—a goal only hoped for by educators in the past, but achievable if we start now.

By knowing the principles and objectives of self-directed learning (SDL), and a variety of ways to help young learners use it, we can give them experiences that stimulate self-reliant learning. Research supports the efficacy of programs for SDL (Guglielmino, 1977; Lane, 1992; Paris, Cross, & Lipson, 1984), but it is not necessary to follow any one pattern or program, because there are many ways to learn.

In a study of the personality characteristics of self-directed learners, University of Georgia's L. M. Guglielmino asked a panel of experts to develop an instrument for assessing an individual's readiness for SDL. The resulting Self-Directed Learning Readiness Scale was administered to 307 participants—high school juniors and seniors, college undergraduates, and adults enrolled in evening noncredit courses. Based on its findings, we can formulate a description of the highly self-directed learner:

> One who exhibits initiative, independence, and persistence in learning; one who accepts responsibility for his or her own learning and views problems as challenges, not obstacles; one who is capable of self-discipline and has a

high degree of curiosity; one who has a strong desire to learn or change and is self-confident; one who is able to use basic study skills, organize his or her time and set an appropriate pace for learning, and to develop a plan for completing work; one who enjoys learning and has a tendency to be goal-oriented. (Guglielmino, 1977, p. 73)

Self-regulated learning strategies have been found to be positively correlated with achievement. Low achievers sometimes use these strategies—checking their work, monitoring their own understanding, asking peers for help—but not in as consistent or determined a manner as do high achievers (Zimmerman & Martinez-Pons, 1986). Teaching students strategies for learning and how to remember what we teach them has a direct, positive effect on academic achievement.

Children enter school with only a vague understanding of what they need to successfully complete academic tasks (Dunn & Dunn, 1979; Meyers & Paris, 1987). They have a limited, intuitive knowledge of strategies (Paris, Lipson, & Wixon, 1983), and as Skinner, Chapman, and Baltes (1988) pointed out, they rarely reflect on their performance. Far too many believe that "trying hard" is sufficient to ensure success (Dweck & Elliott, 1983; Skinner et al., 1988). However, this view changes gradually as children approach adolescence, and their academic self-perceptions become more accurate. Middle school students begin to find out what works best for them and to build a repertoire of skills and strategies that aid learning (Brown & Smiley, 1977; Hartner, 1985; Zimmerman, 1990). Because children's observations and beliefs are often implicit and imprecise, the classroom teacher needs to become involved actively in creating a more formal approach to enhance this process.

Watch any classroom and you will undoubtedly find that all students respond to some degree to the teacher's instruction. But you will also see some students who display initiative, insight, and intrinsic motivation and who take personal responsibility to learn. These are the ones who achieve noteworthy success. Zimmerman (1990) says, "These self-regulated students are distinguished by their systematic use of metacognitive, motivational, and behavioral strategies; by their responsiveness to feedback regarding the effectiveness of their learning; and by their self-perceptions of academic accomplishment" (p. 14). Today, when students appear to lack both the will and skill to achieve schools' standards, teachers need instructional approaches that can offer direction and insight into the skills and processes of SDL.

Some of the observations that Goodlad (1983) noted in his study of schooling were that

> "teacher talk" was by far the dominant classroom activity. Teachers rarely encouraged student-to-student dialog or provided opportunities for students to work collaboratively in small groups or to plan, set goals, determine alternative ways of achieving these goals, and the like. . . . Talking requires the organization of thought and can be an important avenue to learning. . . . Writing even short essays is also conducive to the organization of thoughts and to learning. Students were not doing much of this, either. (pp. 552, 554)

In 1993, the High/Scope Preschool Curriculum Study traced a group of young people through age 27 (Weikart & Schweinhart, 1993), noting the effects of certain preschool curriculum models (Distar, High/Scope, and traditional nursery school models). Until then, most educators had assumed that a high-quality early childhood program could be built on any *theoretically coherent model*. In other words, one model would be as good as another, providing its teachers were quality performers. That study dispelled the notion and led to the conclusion that high-quality preschool curricula are "based on *child-initiated learning activities*" (Schweinhart, Weikart, & Larner, 1986, p. 43; see also Schweinhart, Weikart, & Larner, 1993).

What most traditional classrooms lack are freewheeling thinking and open-ended discussions. In permitting more than one response or way of acting, such activities closely parallel real-life situations (Weikart & Schweinhart, 1993). Students need opportunities to express openly the theories of what they tried to do, how they tried to reach their chosen goals, and what they did when they encountered obstacles. Such verbal exchange with peers allows them to preassess what they will do when faced with similar problems in the future. This type of discussion and analysis may provoke tension and anxiety, but it will also cause a learner to reflect on the need to change his or her *cognitive mapping* (Paris et al., 1984).

Gross and Drabman (1982) found that sixth-grade students can improve behaviors they want to change, through systematic observation and recording of that behavior. The self-directive plan of discipline in this book is based on the premise that teachers and counselors can be more effective if they help intermediate-grade elementary school students identify specific personal behaviors that they wish to change by teaching them how to observe and record that behavior in natural situations.

After the new behavior is established using self-initiated and external reinforcement, teachers will usually find that students do not require or even want external reinforcement to maintain the behavioral change. Apparently, the learner's new understanding and the feedback from self-monitoring the change are sufficient to keep the learner on the selected path.

There is a positive link between high achievement and the use of self-regulated learning strategies (Zimmerman & Martinez-Pons, 1988). An increased repertoire of learning strategies builds a self-confidence that provides maximum learning power. On the other hand, the debilitating effect of a negative self-concept inhibits students' strategic thinking (Corno & Rohrkemper, 1988).

Until students develop a stable sense of positive self-identity reinforced by successful experiences, they cannot engage in the type of self-motivation that can generate the inner drive necessary to be self-directed learners (McCombs, 1986).

People who doubt their capabilities shy away from difficult tasks (Bandura, 1989). To find one's hidden talents and to believe in one's ability enhances self-directed ventures. Although self-knowledge is not all there is to wisdom and maturity, such knowledge makes maturity possible. Yet it is one ingredient that is almost totally neglected when training teachers.

By providing students with ways of getting their own feedback, we can even enhance SDL (Schunk, 1990a). The teacher helps each student identify his or her assets and assigns lessons that promote those findings.

Except for some basic reflexes, people are not born with inborn repertoires of behavior. They must learn them. Likewise, SDL techniques and skills are not inherited—they are learned!

The reason for SDL is survival—of individuals and of humanity. We are not talking about something that would be nice or desirable, or some new educational fad. We are talking about a basic human competence—the ability to learn on one's own—that has become a prerequisite for living in this world.

Questions About Self-Directed Learning

The following questions are often asked by principals who are beginning to explore SDL with their staff and students.

1. *What is self-directed learning?* Students are self-directing to the degree that they actively participate in their own learning processes—*metacognitively, motivationally, and behaviorally* (Zimmerman, 1990). School experiences should be structured so students can teach themselves to control their attention, exhibit some control over their anxiety, and decide what information-processing techniques to use in learning what the teacher has assigned.

SDL requires that students use a form of mental self-government. They receive assistance from principals and teachers, continually refining and using not only what they learn but how they learn.

On a long car trip, you may need a road map—not only to identify the route but perhaps to cut the distance, making the journey more accurate and enjoyable. By analogy, the student needs a cognitive map for the journey through learning—there are a host of *metacognitive processes* to be mapped out in a student's mind during the process of acquiring knowledge. Self-directed learners plan, set goals, self-monitor, and self-evaluate. They select, structure, create, and invent scenarios and environments that maximize learning. They are aware of the relationship between *regulatory processes* (self-efficacy) and strategies to optimize these processes (intermediate goal-setting). They mentally file strategies that they can refer to for achieving learning outcomes. They continually assess whether the strategy used is making them better learners, then alter the strategy or search their cognitive maps for a new one that will help them achieve the desired academic outcome (see Figure 1.1).

2. *How do I recognize self-directed learning?* SDL has the following characteristics:

- *Observable evidence* that a student is taking more responsibility for personalized learning, commensurate with maturational and developmental capabilities. ("As a student, am I working more for internal reasons—pride in my work—than external rewards—stars and grades?")

- *The reality principle* is observable—more real experiences for children, fewer contrived ones. ("How does this information help me to acquire new learning behaviors or change my perceptions for a better self?") The best education is what you learn that helps you successfully manage day-to-day events. Learning experiences should be useful, not just for exercising memory.

- *Respect for natural thinking* is developed. ("Now that I have this information, what can I do with it?") The purpose of learning is to change behavior—mental, emotional, social, physical, academic, psychological. Self-directed learners reconstruct knowledge, extend information, develop theories, make textbooks work for them, and develop new ideas.

- *Teaching occurs on three major levels: facts, thoughts, and intellectual values.* Unless one values what is learned, one rarely retains it. ("What values do I attach to what I've learned today?")

- *Perceptual guidelines* are given for controlling anger-associated behavior and for developing inter- and intrapersonal skills. A student focuses on these ideas: "I can control

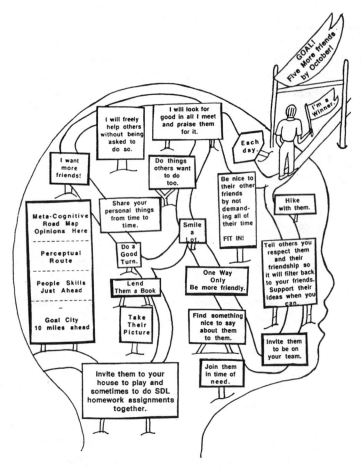

Figure 1.1. Cognitive Map of My Goals
NOTE: A fifth grader used this image of her perceptual route to obtain more friends.

my thoughts; my feelings come from my thoughts; therefore, I can teach myself to control my feelings and actions."

■ *Key processes* are presented by which students can direct how they acquire knowledge. Some activities of
self-directed learners include planning; setting personal
goals; organizing; self-monitoring and self-evaluating;
reconstructing, creating, and inventing ideas; practicing

automaticity; and refining personal skills and behaviors. They repeatedly ask, "What did I do today to delete, amend, or add to my cognitive map?").

3. *Will self-directed learning create a new kind of student?* Yes! Today's technology requires new kinds of students—those who can invent, create, and do abstract thinking on their own without being pushed, prodded, or continuously supervised. Self-directed students see themselves more as owners than as employees on the job, so they not only act different than an ordinary worker, but their work demonstrates a quality and perfection that pleases them, as if they were the owners. Rarely do children in school reflect on their own performance, evaluate themselves, make a plan that ensures success, or even attempt to control their own cognitive abilities. Self-directing schools will develop a series of challenging and achievable goals commensurate with each learner's developmental and maturational traits.

4. *Saying that learners are self-directing implies that there is something else they could be. What are the other choices?* If students do not understand that they have the freedom to learn, they are only a product of conditioning. Such students feel that school controls them; the individual feels shaped by outside forces and experiences. But self-directed students, while recognizing that schools have rules that must be followed, do not turn total control over to the school. Instead, they begin to face the paradox early in life that there are some things outside ourselves over which we have no control, but also a dimension of life over which we do. This dimension—*choice* and *responsibility*—shapes our lives. Self-directed learners can choose what they conform to. Whereas conforming students tend to lack insight into their own motives and may simply go along with the crowd, self-directed learners have good self-understanding and are more independent. They follow rules, seek advice, and conform to policy, but for their own purposes—to get what they need to be better persons. This is why school purposes must match the needs and purposes of students.

5. *If we develop self-directed learners, what behaviors can we expect?* Self-directed learners take pride in getting to and from their classes, lunchrooms, buses, restrooms, and water fountains without much adult supervision. The more you can direct your physical self, the more you feel in charge of your own mind. Lining up to go everywhere in school limits students' feelings of responsibility for self because it establishes the idea that they have little control over their lives.

Self-directed learners see themselves as *owners* of their behavior. They are taught that they are responsible for every act and action. Self-directed learners believe that their feelings come from their thoughts, and if they can control the latter, they can control the former. Teachers who self-direct can help students with their perceptions, thoroughly examining learning principles in each classroom. This internalization process will help students change some old habits and acquire new ones.

6. *Why add self-directed learning to an already overfilled school program?* Because 40% to 50% of our students are not turned on to learning. From middle school up, students tend to become less and less involved with what schools are about. Students say it causes them to live in two separate worlds—the school world and the real world. We do not advocate throwing the baby out with the bath water. SDL does not preclude the values that come from stimulus-response teaching. Instead, we need to structure instructional programs to include both stimulus-response and self-directing theories. Stimulus-response instruction will no longer, by itself, produce learners or leaders for today's world. We have moved from a society in which we were told what to do, to a creative, risk-taking society, seeking more control over our own lives.

7. *Isn't drug abuse by young people a sign that they have been allowed to be too self-directing?* A number of youths who abuse drugs have erroneous information. They believe that taking drugs will solve problems, but they have not been taught to mentally face those problems. Because they tend to believe the outside world caused them to do what they did or be what they are (lonely,

depressed, anxious, angry, unwanted, unskilled), they look for answers in that outside world—alcohol, drugs, promiscuity, pornography, weird cults and religions, even suicide. If their problem was created by the world outside, they reason, why look inward to find the answer?

8. *Give me an example—a perception children hold that ought to be changed. What self-directing understandings will help to change it?* Although schools used to teach about exemplary leaders, a large number of children now believe there are no heroes left. In the media's quest to make things real—to report everything about a situation or person—the private lives of our leaders are fair game. Similarly, new trends in the writing of history tend to stress the realities of violence and exploitation. On the other hand, movies, TV, and popular music offer role models who glorify violence and excitement. The cumulative effect of such imaging affects a student's positive outlook on life. Even middle school youngsters perceive their idols as disdainful of normal life, hard work, and ethics.

But how do we get youngsters to select better heroes as exemplary figures to guide their lives? Children receive a lot of information about the problems they will face in society, but are we giving them any heroes who will help them see how others have handled these problems? Have we helped them perceive how they might become heroes or heroines themselves? Can we discuss what it takes to be strong enough to lead others? A few students already lead exemplary lives. Peers who are well liked can have a strong influence on those around them. Why not start with the local community? Fathers, mothers, grandparents, other relatives, and friends are doing great things right now. Identify who these people are, what they are doing, and the sacrifices they have made to accomplish a chosen goal. Sometimes that is all it takes to tune a youngster in to a wavelength to do something great.

9. *If I encourage children to use SDL techniques, will I be stifling their competitive nature?* No—there is little research to show that human nature is inevitably competitive. Competition has been self-perpetuating—each generation is taught that it has

no choice but to compete, from Little League to science fairs. To the contrary, we believe we need to teach children to run against their own "stopwatches"—to know they are smarter today than they were yesterday; to know that they solve something faster today than they did the day before; or to see that it takes less time now to prepare for a test than it took 3 weeks ago.

These comparisons of self-achievement are much more important to the learner. How long would you run in a race if every time you ran, you lost? But knowing that you ran a few seconds faster today than yesterday, that you beat your own record, is better than to run and always lose.

When you run against your own stopwatch, any improvement is directly observable. SDL calls for intrapersonal competition—setting standards and goals, predicting speeds of finishing work, gauging quality of responses, and measuring and evaluating progress. The student intends to beat his own mark or surpass his previous performance by using intelligent practice and unyielding commitment. The attitude to be a winner comes from within. However, if the learning environment is structured for competition, the motivation to win comes from outside, a win/lose situation. Something else may be motivating him—the coach, a cheering crowd, or glittering awards. If we see the learner as a self-regulating feedback system, we must give him the information and perceptual skills to judge and operate his personalized system of *behaviors* and *specialized skills*. This is competition at its best.

Exposing the Myths About Self-Directed Learning

In visiting with educators and reviewing the literature over the past decade, we have encountered a number of myths or misconceptions regarding SDL. These myths have often added to the confusion over the meaning of SDL and its implications as a classroom educational practice. We will try here to identify and correct these myths.

Myth 1: In self-directed learning, schools are turned over to the children. Nothing is further from the truth! Teachers are needed more, not less. A facilitating teacher continuously monitors a student's personal perceptions of learning, offering opportunities to learn new strategies, providing feedback, and assisting the student in developing the perceptions to serve as an ethical base to guide his or her life.

Myth 2: Self-direction is a philosophy that emphasizes personal responsibility for learning—the words sound good, but can never be achieved. Only the latter part is a myth. Until we tap the initiative of learners, they will always lean more on teachers than on themselves. Self-directed learners learn, with teacher help, how to diagnose their own needs, make a plan of action, and then carry out the plan themselves. They are encouraged to ask for help along the way if needed.

Lane's (1992) study revealed that SDL students increased retention, had a greater variety of interests, had more positive attitudes toward the learning situation, and had a systematic way of learning what was prescribed. In fact, students in the experimental group learned, per person, 2½ times more strategies for learning purposes than the control group that had not been encouraged to develop learning strategies.

Myth 3: School rules will be violated because students can roam about at will. On the contrary, school rules take on a new flavor. A youngster immersed in SDL perceptions realizes that he is responsible for his every act. Thus, he stops blaming the school for doling out punishment and gets his own act in order. There are time periods set for strengthening self-directive behaviors, and places in the school are identified where children can go on their own without strict supervision by adults. Students take pride in moving about the school in business-like fashion. They appreciate this type of trust and rarely abuse it.

Myth 4: Self-directed learning is just more commercial, "packaged" learning that a student contracts for and does at his or her own speed. Commercial packages usually deal with academic content, whereas SDL deals more with assessing and developing students' inner perceptions. They are encouraged to look within to see *how* they know *what* they know. If you change the perceptions of the students toward themselves, school, and learning, you have a more powerful set of learners.

A wide variety of learning activities and approaches are used to encourage students to take personal responsibility for their own learning. They develop strategies for learning and practice them until they are automatic. Although commercial packages may still be used, they are not blindly assigned for student use irrespective of needs. Instead, a package is chosen because formal preassessment suggests certain skills that the youngster needs to practice systematically.

Myth 5: Self-directed learning is for more able students with higher IQs and for those who come from middle- and upper-income families. Lane's (1992) investigation revealed that children of middle and lower levels of intelligence acquired an equal number of strategies for learning as did students with higher IQs. It is conceivable that a person with a high IQ, who has acquired self-directing skills, will be able to reach a higher level of performance, but this does not mean that bright students automatically acquire self-directing behaviors and skills without training. Because we believe that "intelligence is learned," we use IQ tests only to compare where a student appears to be functioning without SDL experiences. It seems to be a good basis for determining the level at which a student is using intellectual skills.

Myth 6: Teachers can no longer use large groups (the whole class) for instruction. In our experience in regular classrooms, large group size need not deter the use of self-directing approaches. However, lesson plans should include working with classes in ways different from the typical lecture format, and settings where teachers talk for a few minutes, then ask the kids some questions about "facts." One suggestion is to move gradually from straight lecturing to lecturing in 3-minute episodes, after which the teacher and class spend 2 to 3 minutes discussing, "How are you going to remember what I'm teaching you?" This procedure would not be needed every day, but would balance lecture and learning techniques. At other times, break large groups into smaller groups using cooperative learning techniques.

Myth 7: Letting students choose what they will learn and how they will learn it will erode sequential learning and the systematic steps of teaching that are essential to the teaching-learning process. It is true that young children will need a lot of teacher guidance in choosing options to help them learn what is being taught. And it is also probable that some children, until they learn better, will take advantage of the freedom given them. Perhaps therein lies the problem. If freedoms are *earned,* instead of given, students can be eased into understanding self-directing principles and gradually weaned away from traditional forms of teaching. As their individual initiative increases, the greater the number of self-directing activities they are allowed to assume. So it is a myth to believe that learning is turned over to the student and the teacher sits back and does nothing. When children learn that you expect them to become more responsible for school learning, they work to fulfill maximum requirements (usually their own goals), instead of settling for minimum requirements set by their teacher.

Myth 8: Schools have to set goals; most elementary and inter-mediate level children are not mature enough—cognitively, psychologically, or intellectually—to do so, or to know the steps essential to wise goal setting. It is granted that goal setting needs to be done cooperatively and that children need a teacher's exper-tise. But goals for students should not be set before the students arrive—they need to be involved, along with teachers. Not long ago, a school violated this principle. Using the President's Physi-cal Education Program for the first time, instead of following the provided guidelines, some classrooms were allowed to set personal goals and choose the number of calisthenics they would do. Some first graders wound up with aching sides and had to be checked by a doctor because they chose to do as many as they could. Goals set by students should come under the guidance of their teachers. Remember, when you help youngsters understand their roles in school and society, they will set more reasonable goals. If students do not know where their academic goalposts are, how will they know when they have scored academic touchdowns? Daily and weekly personal and academic goals should be identified, discussed, and written down for guidance purposes.

Myth 9: Self-directed learning is just a fad. Of the many myths surrounding SDL, one thing is certain—*SDL is not a fad.* Most people use facets of it every day (Brockett & Hiemstra, 1991). Once it is understood by the learner, it becomes a tremendous motivating force in subsequent learning and implementation of perceptual behavior. To learn something from someone else is rewarding, but to learn it yourself is often viewed as something close to a miracle.

Self-directed learners amass perceptions and skills that will benefit them for a lifetime. Advanced technology not only promotes but requires SDL skills. In the near future, evaluating the effectiveness of a school will require determining the extent to which its program helps students use self-directing perceptions and processes. Historically, most teachers have believed they should help students control for *output* as measured on teacher-made tests, standardized exams, and homework assignments. We believe, however, that the greatest help to students is controlling *input*—acquiring ideas that will increase personal perceptual powers. This is the type of learning that changes behaviors, develops meaning and values from academic content, and provides the student with a chance to observe his own inner nature. The student who learns to look *within* for meaning will take in more of what the school has to offer.

2 Self-Directing Versus Traditional Schools

What's the Difference?

The traditional school, immersed in stimulus-response theory, served its clients well when families stayed together, educators had discipline power, less violence appeared on television, and more students made an effort to learn. But now teaching is harder than ever. In spite of the great number of dedicated teachers who are committed to doing the best job within their power, even the best of them are confronted daily with increasing numbers of students who make little or no effort to learn (Glasser, 1986).

If we are to continue to reach children who are already turned on to learning (about half of them), to entice another 25% to 30% to want to learn, and perhaps still another 10% along the way, we have got to make schools more satisfying. A self-directing school helps students achieve some preset goals immediately, which not only gives them a feeling of accomplishment but also makes schools satisfying. Students will keep working, even on unimportant things, if they feel some personal satisfaction, if what they are doing makes sense to them. We have not yet trusted children enough to give them a major role in choosing what to learn, how to learn it, and to act responsibly by creating a personal plan for achieving certain standards and goals.

Two Approaches to Learning

Once learners grasp the meaning of SDL, they get ready to take the initiative, with or without help, in diagnosing their learning needs, formulating learning goals, identifying human and material resources to aid in the quest, choosing and implementing appropriate learning skills and strategies, and evaluating her own learning outcomes. SDL is not something learners do in isolation; it requires various helpers, such as mentors, tutors, resource people, peers—and *teachers*! A brief look at self-directed learners in action will show a lot of sharing of materials, ideas, and assisting each other (see Table 2.1).

What Competencies Must a Student Have to Be a Good Self-Directed Learner?

The traditional competencies required to excel in teacher-directed learning, as every A student will tell you, include the ability to listen attentively, to take careful notes, to read fast and with good comprehension, and to predict exam questions. Aren't these really the ones we have come to rely on in school? SDL, however, requires a very different set of competencies, as noted in Figure 2.1.

These competencies do not refer to permissive teaching in which students run wild with whatever thoughts enter their minds. Instead, they indicate a creativity that teaches students self-discipline, not just to please their teachers, but so they can discover, with supervision, the most effective ways to conduct their own lives. Creative and risk-taking students cannot be confined by the rules of the general classroom. The more teachers permit students to bend the rules, experiment with new approaches to learning, try out unique ideas, negotiate homework,

TABLE 2.1 Self-Directed and Teacher-Directed Learning

Self-Directed	*Teacher Directed*
1. Recognizes that the student grows in intellectual and psychological capacity to be self-directing and has an innate need to exercise control over his or her life. This capacity and need should be nurtured to develop more over time.	1. Assumes the student is essentially dependent. Thus, the teacher has the responsibility of deciding what is to be taught and when and how.
2. Believes that as a learner grows in experience, he or she becomes a major resource for determining future learning, and this should be used along with textbooks and other resources.	2. Depicts the student's experience as less valuable than the teacher's, so the teacher "calls the shots" without student input. Sees textbook authors as major resources and tries to transmit their ideas to the learner's mind.
3. Contends that learners are so individual in development that each is ready to learn what is essential to perform his or her life tasks and that they need a plan to deal with the daily problems of living.	3. Accepts the view that students mature at varying rates, but at times have common characteristics and learning needs and can be grouped for teaching purposes.
4. Declares that subject matter orientation stifles learner initiative and that the natural way of learning immerses students in problem-centered experiences, personal projects, and current needs, thus helping them master daily problems.	4. Claims that students, especially older ones, have a subject-centered orientation to learning. Their learning experiences are organized according to the respective disciplines—lessons, units, and tests become the focal point of teaching.
5. Postulates the view that *internal* incentives—native curiosity, the need for self-esteem, the challenge of power, and the satisfaction of accomplishment—and *fulfillment* are better motivators of student accomplishment.	5. Believes that students need *external* incentives to learn; that punishment and force may be needed to keep kids on the task; and if all else fails, grades and diplomas will keep students learning.

or develop plans for guiding their life at school, the more they will foster the creative spirit.

Competency	*I demonstrate these . . . (0 = never, 1 = seldom, 2 = often, and 3 = very often)*
1. A concept of myself being more in charge of my life.	0___ 1___ 2___ 3___
2. The ability to diagnose my learning needs realistically, with school help (teachers, peers, and prescribed materials).	0___ 1___ 2___ 3___
3. Ability to see the difference between expecting my teacher to make me learn and my own power to direct myself to learn and to expect results without being forced to perform (by principal, teacher, parents, and peers).	0___ 1___ 2___ 3___
4. Ability to use peers as helpers and encouragers with my learning needs, instead of as doers of my work.	0___ 1___ 2___ 3___
5. Ability to transform my learning needs into learning behaviors and objectives. I can identify these behaviors and practice them.	0___ 1___ 2___ 3___
6. Ability to identify effective learning strategies and perform them with a reasonable degree of skill.	0___ 1___ 2___ 3___
7. Ability to identify material resources for information to help carry out my chosen objectives.	0___ 1___ 2___ 3___
8. Ability to collect personal evidence to verify my achievements of personal goals and school prescribed objectives.	0___ 1___ 2___ 3___
9. Ability to motivate myself to do what I should, without external incentives, school rules, or adult pressure to do the prescribed work.	0___ 1___ 2___ 3___

Figure 2.1. Self-Rating the Competencies for Self-Directed Learning

Competency	I demonstrate these . . . (0 = never, 1 = seldom, 2 = often, and 3 = very often)
10. Ability to use the skills of appropriate and equivalent practice effectively in refining previous behaviors and skills.	0___ 1___ 2___ 3___
11. Ability to increase my reading rate by concentrating on the number of words my eyes take in during one fixation on a page.	0___ 1___ 2___ 3___
12. Ability to improve note taking during lectures by jotting ideas around a center instead of linear notes.	0___ 1___ 2___ 3___

Figure 2.1. Continued

Think about this question: If each student learns only to perform like everybody else, what does an individual student really have to offer himself? an employer? society?

Native Curiosity and Traditional Teaching

Teachers for a long time have assumed that pupils will automatically use their innate capabilities. One has only to watch 4- to 7-year-olds for a few minutes to discover that the very young are self-starters and will work on something with very little encouragement from their teachers. Kindergartners and first graders demonstrate an eagerness for action; they want to find out, explore, and engage in novel activities.

But as students go through school, their inner motivations change due to external stimuli. Less self-directed children have been found to receive an average of 17 task-directing sentences per hour from their teachers; by contrast, highly self-directed children receive an average of just two sentences per hour (Biemiller & Meichenbaum,

TABLE 2.2 Roles of Self-Directing and Traditional Teachers

Self-Directing Teacher Role	Traditional Teacher Role
1. Involves students in planning	1. Sets up class her way
2. Assigns lessons according to learners' developmental needs	2. Gives all students the same assignments
3. Students set personal standards they can reach	3. Predetermines goals for entire class
4. Most tests require students to demonstrate knowledge and skill	4. Most tests are paper-and-pencil type
5. Learning for long-term, chosen purposes	5. Memorization for memory's sake
6. Reading for depth, to unlock meaning	6. Reading for mechanical purposes, to unlock words
7. Students are taught to become responsible for their actions	7. Discipline is dominant
8. Teaching is demonstrating	8. Teaching is telling
9. Teaching is assessing the best way to learn	9. Teaching is making assignments
10. Teaching is giving deserved freedoms	10. Teaching is controlling
11. Knowledge is seen as power (and higher grades come naturally)	11. Knowledge is seen as academic achievement
12. Teacher is modern manager	12. Teacher is boss
13. Teachers and students look for what needs to be changed; they see the future as opportunity to acquire new ideas	13. Teachers see future as more of the same
14. Students monitor their own behaviors, then move about properly by themselves with limited supervision	14. Teacher marches students to lunchroom, in and out of building
15. Student perceptions are monitored and regular lessons offered to help them take control of their lives	15. No formal attempt to change students' perceptions or attitudes

1992). This suggests that teachers and peers often "think for" the less self-directed students (see Table 2.2). Pupils soon begin the road of least resistance, where attendance records and grades become the statistical mileposts of progress.

In schools where the curriculum is prescribed before students arrive, and where teachers do things to and for them, instructors become a kind of intellectual crutch for learners. But in schools where the burden of responsibility is shifted to the learners' shoulders, pupils begin once again to use their own self-propulsion.

Do Schools Stifle Self-Directing Behavior?

In a Canadian study, some walleyed pikes were put in a tank, then fed minnows, their natural food. The next time the pikes were hungry, the researchers placed thick glass between the pikes and the minnows. The pikes charged at full speed toward the minnows, hitting the glass the first time with a real thump. The next time, they did it again, but at a reduced speed. On the average, the pikes hit the glass seven times, each time a little slower. Finally, they would just float up to the glass, eat the other food around, and watch the minnows. After 9 to 10 days, they would ignore the minnows, even when the glass was removed. Their natural behavior had been extinguished.

Analogously, children are like the walleyed pikes—they will try to do what the school wants for just so long, then if they are not successful, they will give up and not try anymore. They feel unsuccessful; their test scores tell them they are unsuccessful. So they cease to do more than minimal performance. Their inability to cope has destroyed their motivation, feelings of adequacy, and zeal to please themselves and others.

It is not schools alone that cause the reduction of self-initiated learning. The home and family play a big part in a child's willingness and ability to become self-directing. Too often parents give children material things that the children do not have to work for. Why work for something that is simply handed to you if you fuss?

How Must Teachers Change?

Most teachers have been trained as you were—listing the content to be covered in a given discipline (concepts, principles, theories, facts, and skills), jotting page numbers and things to be done in their plan books. They probably give more time to what is to be covered than what is to be learned. They organize content into manageable units (daily lessons, weekly units, semester goals), decide how to transmit it (lecture, discussion, videos), and devise strategies for measuring what was transmitted.

SDL strategies will fail if a teacher expects her youngsters to change, while she performs the same way. The self-directing teacher involves her students in all decisions that affect them, from determining what is to be learned to when it is to be taught, and for what purposes. Some teachers who are changing over to SDL strategies are shocked when they discover that some of their students do not want to be self-directed learners—they would rather have everything done for them and dished out on a platter!

Teachers will no longer be just imparters of information but facilitators. The traditional role allowed the teacher to focus on how well she transmitted information. But the facilitator role requires the teacher to focus on the learner—not only how he feels about what he's learning, but how what he's learning is helping him right now. This type of dialogue with a student can turn out to be a very humbling experience.

SDL requires the teacher to have personal, caring, meaningful contacts with each student. The teacher must remove the traditional protective shield of an authority figure and become more open in communication with students (Table 2.3)

Emphasize the Value of Schooling

Teachers do not talk enough about the real benefits of education. Studying should be done for the internal benefits it gives students, not for some external reward like an A on a report card. Children should believe, "A lot of sound information and knowledge can make me a powerful person." Do not emphasize

TABLE 2.3 Self-Directing and Traditional Teachers: What Teachers Should and Should Not Do

Teachers Should	Teachers Should Not
1. Be more able to listen to students, especially to words that depict the learner's feelings	1. Give too many answers
2. Be better able to accept students' innovative, challenging, "troublesome," creative ideas, rather than reacting to these threats by insisting on conformity	2. Demonstrate behaviors that show they are not in charge of their own stressors and emotions
3. Tend to pay as much attention to the relationship with students as to the content of the course	3. Apply only school rules and seldom, if ever, involve students in individual and group discussions that lead to self-discipline principles and techniques
4. Be more likely to work out interpersonal frictions and problems with students, rather than deal with such issues in a disciplinary or punitive manner	4. Dominate and control all physical movements of students, no matter where they are in the building
5. Develop a more egalitarian atmosphere in the classroom, conducive to spontaneity, creative thinking, and to self-directed work (Rogers, 1969)	5. Give a single assignment to the whole class and fail to personalize learning by giving students choices and options in what to do
	6. Emphasize subject matter achievement, on one hand, and neglect to assess students' personal perceptual change, on the other
	7. Lecture most of the time, or repeatedly use a routine pattern of questioning one student after another
	8. Focus on educational analysis of students' learning ability and environments as fixed or stable traits. (Ability is made up of skills, and it typically increases with experience.)
	9. Compare a student's performance to that of others. (Students should have an opportunity to run against their own academic stopwatches. Comparing a student with another puts the control of his or her life in other hands, rather than the student's own. Overly competitive students often determine their own worth by looking at the performance of others. This is neither fair nor wise.)
	10. Be inflexible about retaining and failing kids. (We learn very little by success. To experience the exhilaration of success, self-directing students must learn how to profit from failure. In 1927, Babe Ruth hit 60 home runs. But that same year he also struck out more than anyone in baseball. It's simple—if you want to hit home runs, you have to be willing to swing at strikes! Self-directing kids seem to understand that there is a great difference between failing at a task and being a failure as a person. In a self-directing school, the individual chooses his own goals, so they will be realistic, motivating, educationally sound, and achievable.)

25

long-range goals that are impersonal or meaningless to students. To tell a first grader that he needs to make high grades so he can get into college is ludicrous. You can help first graders more by talking positively about what they are doing now; help them to develop good attitudes toward school and the joy that comes from knowing that you know more today than you did yesterday. Let long-range goals take care of themselves.

If a child develops a love of learning on a day-to-day basis, what he does on a daily basis is what counts. Children will decide for themselves about going to college. If they do, the decision will be based on whether they like school, the daily study habits they have developed, their own perceptions 12 years from now, economic conditions at that time, and dozens of other factors. Each of us works best on the goals we have chosen for ourselves, goals we can reach and that give us feelings of fulfillment. Students need personal goals they can achieve right away, the successful completion of which will vault them into setting other attainable goals.

What SDL Facilitators Should Know

1. Students need personal intellectual standards if they are to direct their own thinking and understand the thinking of others.

2. Because we are always in the process of learning, becoming educated means we have acquired the ability to gather, analyze, synthesize, evaluate, and apply information for ourselves.

3. The depth of a student's thinking is more important than how much of the curriculum has been covered. Although students have obtained reading skills, if they do not have the intellectual ability to guide themselves to read what they should, reading has lost its power in their lives. It is just as serious when students are not reading material at the depth they are capable of as it is when they are not able to read at all.

4. Students value what they learn and give their time to *after* school. Students who are often in trouble in school because they have not acquired the value systems against which they are being judged need school help to acquire and master the knowledge and skills that will help them to adjust in social settings. Learning that one is responsible for obtaining one's own ethical and aesthetic value system, and discovering that school can help provide direction, is an important part of SDL.

5. What students think about when receiving feedback from others and how they perceive themselves is what they become. Self-directed students must learn how to transform themselves into what they are capable of becoming. A self-directed person's philosophy becomes "What I am to be is up to me!"

6. Teachers cannot give students knowledge—only information and data. Knowledge is acquired only through thinking, so self-directed students should be questioned regularly to determine how they are using the information they have received.

7. Students who can tell what they believe and why are those who are more likely going to change when they see something better. Self-reflection opens the mind's pathway to improved self-direction.

8. Unless learners realize that they are formulating a system for all subsequent learning, they will not try to refine how they learn things, to control what their minds take in, or attempt to use the information for developing a better self. Self-directed students grow cognitively to realize that all learning behaviors (physical, mental, emotional, social) are to help change oneself into a more fulfilling, functioning, joyous human being.

9. Student exchange—listening, talking, teaching others— that is focused on live issues and mutual needs is a top sign of learning. Active learning takes precedence over passively accepting whatever the teacher says.

10. A self-directed learner plans, sets goals, self-monitors, and self-evaluates at various points during the process of acquiring skills and knowledge. Once self-directed learners are aware of new information, they take the necessary steps to master it.

11. Students who self-regulate and self-direct learn to depend on feedback to monitor their learning effectiveness. The feedback itself is reward enough to continue their efforts; external rewards seem to be of secondary importance.

12. Successful and unsuccessful learners differ in their orientations to school, in their motivation to advance their knowledge, and in knowing appropriate strategies for success. Unfortunately, at around 12 years old, a number of students begin to believe that people have a fixed amount of intelligence that remains unaltered by the amount of effort a learner puts forth. This is contrary to the self-directing principle that all learners can set their own goals and standards, because *intelligence is learned*. Successful students are motivated by internal standards because they believe they can extend their intelligence, whereas less successful students are more oriented to extrinsic rewards and social controls.

The teacher who helps a student become self-directing will help the students to

- Gain knowledge and the student's own memory processes (metamemory);
- Gain skill in the use of personalized thinking processes (metacognition); and,
- Become familiar with processing information, determining alternative learning strategies, and selecting the best strategy for the situation (executive processes). Students who can *perceive* what they know about knowing, and how they know it, can gain more through studying than can students who follow traditional modes.

3 Looking at Self-Directed Learners

To see what others could tell us about the value of SDL, we turned to the experts—the people who use it. These responses are real. We saw them happen, and in some instances, made them happen. They will show what can happen—children do not lie about these things. We hope their stories will provide both practical answers and inspiration. (The children's names have been changed to protect their privacy.)

Carla, Grade 5

I've never liked school since second grade because I always felt dumb. One day when Dr. B. came in, he put up a sign that read, "Intelligence is learned!" And then he recited a cute little poem about "making a better you."

Believe it or not, big dumb me never had to look at that poem again. I was so surprised. He says you have to hear and see it immediately for storage in your mind and then he gives you a minute to write your notes in three or four ways—network it, draw a picture, write down key words.

I wanted the poem and I was going to ask to see it so I could copy it. Then I found myself writing it from memory! I checked it against his—I was exactly right. I told it to my parents. I saw it in my imaging that I practice each night. I woke up once and said it in my mind. I know it by heart.

I love SDL. I'm smarter now than I was before this project. In SDL I can make mistakes and no one knows about them but my teacher. And he doesn't mind—he'll just say, "Wow! Another golden opportunity for you—you now know better what to do!" And funny thing is, I really do! You know what? I'm not so dumb. Don't laugh, I just might be a teacher.

John, Grade 5

John was having a difficult time in class although he was working hard. He was a nice boy at times, but seemed almost burned out. On the Bradley-Lane Self-Directing Perceptual Scale (Lane, 1996), John checked items such as "I set goals that are easy so I can accomplish them with little effort," and "I don't tell people my ideas because they will laugh." Most of John's answers were negative.

Although he did not like to work out all of our assignments, John liked mathematical games, so we negotiated. If he would find some games to put on the blackboard, we would consider this as one activity to meet that obligation. Second, if he would submit a game 2 days ahead that matched an assignment in our projects, these could be his suggested strategies for learning the textbook math. I assured him that if he taught the class a math game, the children would like it, not laugh at him, and see he was a responsible person willing to help them learn how to enjoy math. He seemed to like this, and with the thought that he would really be helping, John became an eager contributor.

He began bringing problems to class and seemed to thrive on the responses of his classmates, who began to think he was a genius in math. He read the math lesson to see what types of problems it contained. Each day, I would let him present three short problems to the class.

John's life took an interesting turn. He began to do his math as quickly as he could, because when he completed it first, I would let him put the next day's problem on the board. Before class began, he would give help where needed. Some students asked to see additional problems we did not use in class. He mimeographed problems. He made up problems. He asked Sheila, our best art student, to draw a few simple pictures to illustrate some of his tricky problems to help others see the possibilities. His whole attitude seemed to change by doing something profitable for himself in school.

Although John did not achieve perfection in the project, he did improve. His work habits increased favorably, and he seemed better liked by his peers. Students thought his math problems were fun and caused them to think in ways the regular math did not. He took pride in his sharing with the math class, and it was evident that his self-concept improved between his first presentation and the last one several weeks later. He said, "I'm getting a better grade in math class now and am doing better in social studies. I'm going to set a new goal there too—I'm going to study famous generals on my own and my teacher says I can share it with our class."

Diane, Grade 4

Diane did all of the work the teacher assigned, always asking if it would be on the next test. She seemed to lack initiative to do much on her own. When she finished her work, she would just sit. When the teacher asked if she would like to go to the library, she said, "What for? I've done my work already." Her responses in class were accurate, but couched in terms like, "This is what the book says." What does a self-directing teacher do for students like Diane?

(*Diane's teacher*) I held 5-minute sessions with Diane for 5 weeks, as well as some extra time when I had it. I talked about the fact that some women don't take enough initiative in society, developing their personal power or becoming a part of the working world as they are capable of doing. When I asked Diane if she was happy and being all she could be, I seemed to capture her attention. She said she "hadn't really thought about it," but I could tell it was a question she hadn't heard before. We talked about taking risks, and I brought her some clippings about women in the workforce, who had found they had to be better at certain job skills than men if they were in competition for a job. We talked about doing things for yourself, not relying on others.

The third week, Diane consented to an extra assignment. She took the responsibility of making a bulletin board on unique jobs held by women—a mayor, a powder-puff derby racer, a sky diver. After she started, several female classmates also brought her articles. Diane then asked the teacher next door if she would have her girls collect some items too. The board grew and had to be expanded to the hallway. I put Diane's school picture beside her work, listing a few positive things about her.

Diane began to change. She is more active now in class. She has evidently discovered a connection between school assignments and what they mean to learning. She communicates pleasantly with others now and helps them from time to time. She seems interested in more and has taken more interest in her personal appearance.

Diane's questions have changed from "What's going to be on the test?" to the recent "Will you please edit my paper so it will be correct in case the editor selects it for the school newspaper?" Diane is now participating and thinking—responding not only to my suggestions but to several of her own inner needs and observations.

SDL is a good vehicle to use to get children to recognize learning is to be *an active personal experience and you only get out of it what you are willing to put into it.* A critic might say, "You can get kids to learn without using self-directing experiences." Yes, that's possible. But when the carrot is gone, does the mule move very much? We doubt it. On the other hand, when a student develops perceptions such as Diane's, and consciously uses them in daily life, she generally continues to work and learn when neither a teacher nor parents are around.

> (*Diane's perceptions*) First, when I practice skills on my own, making them automatic, I also learn more new ideas when the teacher is teaching.
>
> Second, my perceptions tell me who and what I am. I can be anything I want to be—I just have to start doing what I need to do. I can't dream all the time—I finally have to decide to do something.
>
> Third, if you try to become something that will make you a better person, it's impossible to be a total failure.
>
> Fourth, it's also impossible to succeed perfectly. Some improvement is better than none.
>
> Fifth, *now* is the time to think about what you can be. It's easier to change now than to try to change later in life. Anyone can be better if they choose, and if they try.

Cleveland, Grade 6

Cleveland, a "super learner," seemed intrigued with the information about improving reading speed. To improve speed, one must first be able to read general words at an average speed (fifth-grade average, 60-90 words per minute). Cleveland was taught how to take his own reading rate, and we suggested that he do this for a month, at about the same time of day in a quiet place. His preassessment revealed that he was a typical reader, picking up only one word per fixation in silent reading. Even if he could not pick up additional words as a sixth grader, in a year or two he would be reading faster.

Cleveland started with a reading rate of 80 words per minute and by the end of 30 days, had reached 120 words per minute. For 3 months, he continued testing his rate on his own, and his last report was 149 words per minute. Evidently, at least two things happened in Cleveland's reading experiment. Practicing improved Cleveland's rate anyway, but his metacognitive level told him, "Pick up another word, read faster—you can do it!" During the experiment, the serendipitous effect on Cleveland's self-esteem was exciting to see. He had something no one else had; in fact, he had done something even he did not believe he could do. Moreover, Cleveland said, "Some people who hadn't ever talked to me before, or asked for my help, wanted me to show them what I was doing. I taught eight classmates how to do speed tests. They thought I was smart! How about that?"

Tiffany and Lindsey, Grade 3

The self-directing principle says, "To qualify as a self-directed learner, one must be able to extend the skills learned in school, using them in practical and creative ways." Third graders Tiffany and Lindsey gave us samples of their original stories, which are published regularly in their local newspaper. The girls write a story a week in their classroom. Lindsey has always read a lot, but now she reaches in many directions, using ideas she finds elsewhere to help create them. Tiffany, as a result of her new writing skills, says, "I now read much more widely—to be a good writer, you have to know a great number of good ideas to capture your readers' interest." Lindsey agrees. "Knowing a lot helps, but ideas aren't enough—you have to put them a new way so a reader likes your new twist to a story."

Each girl remarked that she knew her own self-discipline had made her a good writer. With their teacher's help, they became so inner motivated that their skills are now automatic and do not get in the way of their writing—they can concentrate on the story itself. This is what SDL is all about—refining and extending acquired skills.

Their teacher did more than teach writing skills effectively— she encouraged other students to become more self-directing too. It is evident that their skills transfer to papers they have written in other subjects. She opens avenues for her youngsters beyond the actual classroom, reminds them of deadlines, and sees that their work is presented elsewhere. This is another example of what self-directing teachers do for their learners.

Billy, Grade 4

(*Billy's teacher*) Billy was perhaps the smartest student in the fourth grade. He lived at the Children's Home and came from a broken family. Behavior was a concern from the first day of class. He would speak out of turn, provoke aggressive behavior on the playground, and generally disrupt the class at any given moment. I could reason with him after an incident, but the long-range effect seemed minimal. We would make a plan and then immediately have to make another. Helping with other students gave him a lift and then he would want to do more to help in class.

We composed a checklist to help him monitor his behavior. Just before class was dismissed each day, we would go over the list to see if he had addressed them. A blank in the space meant he had not demonstrated that behavior satisfactorily. A check meant that he had tried, but had not quite reached his goal. A plus sign meant he was successful. If he had more than two blanks a day, he received demerits at the home.

The day would start off on a rocky footing. He might be belligerent, arrogant, and disrespectful. After an hour or so, he would modify his behavior to conform to the rules. At the end of the day, we would go over the behaviors together and decide how he had done. If he had done well in the afternoon, but not in the morning, he thought he should be given credit for his actions. He began to realize that he was responsible for his behavior all day and that he needed to start the day in a positive frame of mind to be successful. It took almost a school year for him to understand that he alone is responsible for his behavior.

Billy, an exceptionally talented writer, can spin off a story quickly. If his ability is mentioned by his classmates, it increases his self-esteem. The other students like his stories and look to him as a leader, but if he does not receive this attention, his disruptive side comes out. On the playground, he is aggressively competitive. He reacts without thinking and sometimes kicks, hits, or shoves other children, often calling them names as well. By becoming aware of his aggressive behavior, he has come to deal with it. He may decide not to play a game because he knows he may lose his temper. Instead of playing soccer, he may decide to shoot baskets by himself. There are some days when he seems unable to handle the daily tasks. On those days, I may call him aside and ask how his day is going. When he understands that he must contain himself and accept certain conditions in life, it is easier for him to bring the appropriate behavior to the surface.

A Look at the Evidence

These case histories support the view that a developmentally appropriate, self-directing program fosters students' willingness to extend classroom assignments and personal choices to a higher level of performance. Each student seemed to feel empowered to use more personal initiative, which promoted inquisitiveness about people, things, and ideas. These students really charted new paths for themselves in their learning processes.

During the Lane (1992) study, which emphasized teacher collaboration and negotiation with students on curriculum, learning strategies, and personalized evaluation techniques, a fifth grader remarked that such choices "lead to thinking and acting, rather than just memorizing and remembering." The evidence supporting that view is so compelling that it is difficult to understand how any educator can talk about school reform without addressing how students can be given more say in their classes.

There also seems to be a serendipitous effect on the learner's behavior. If a teacher tells a student what to do and how to do it, and it does not work, the student is ready to give up, rarely trying it another way and often blaming the teacher. But if students start something on their own and discover they cannot finish it that way, they will usually stop and try another way, feeling sure that this time they will be more successful.

The Experts Speak

Assessing the Research

Maria M. Shelton, Program Dean
National Ed.D. Program for Educational Leaders
NOVA Southeastern University
Fort Lauderdale, Florida
Past President, Professors of Elementary and Middle School
Administrators
Past President, NCPEA

In assessing the research on SDL, I found that

■ Self-directing behaviors are learned;
■ Assisting students with developing their own perceptions is just as important to learning as academic subjects;
■ Self-directed students become more highly motivated than students who do only what they are assigned; and
■ It is important to look at SDL from a lifelong perspective.

By getting children to change how they think about their behavior, teachers can help them change how they act in class, and this positive change carries over into their experiences outside school. The long-term effects of SDL show that children who are taught to tackle their own behavior problems do change. SDL strategies emphasize the student's responsibility to treat others with respect and to develop the individual's capacity for self-instruction. Self-directed learners learn how to change their perceptions to change their behaviors.

Asian teachers and parents often view success in school as a direct result of effort, whereas Americans tend to relate such success to natural ability. We can do little to change innate ability, but we can do much to increase each student's degree of effort as, simultaneously, we teach them the self-directing skills that are essential to improving performance.

SDL perspectives are a "must" part of the personalized education program for females. For girls to establish a niche on which to build additional cognitive powers to acquire their chosen roles, they must move from being led by others to achieve preset goals. The self-directed female student has a better chance of becoming what she wants to by being more assertive, more demanding of her rights, and more of a visionary than heretofore allowed to be.

SDL philosophy and the skills it produces are essential to student empowerment. *Adult control cannot be the goal.* The new goal has to be a trust that given the opportunity, students will exercise more control over themselves—personally and educationally. There are structural, attitudinal, cultural, and program barriers erected by enough educators (teachers, principals, and others) to seem nearly impregnable. Unless SDL principles are soon implemented in schools, students will continue to feel hopeless, helpless, and powerless—and so will some of the adults who teach them. The time has come in education to recognize that stimulus-response theory is not the only way to achieve the best conditions for learning. It must be supplemented (and sometimes replaced) with self-directing instructional and educational experiences of the highest order.

Basic Requirements for Successful Schools

Barbara McPherson, Principal
Stony Point North Elementary School
Kansas City, Kansas

For some time, I have been implementing the philosophy of SDL among my students and building staff. For example, at our annual science fair, all projects from Grades 1 to 5 are based on cooperative group efforts, thus giving students the opportunity to direct their learning and projects. A science assessment is required in fifth grade, but we don't use the traditional question/answer format. Instead, students are placed in groups that must cooperatively solve the problem, then document their results. They receive both a team and an individual score.

The following are examples of strategies that have assisted us in making our students more self-directing, self-motivated, and self-sufficient.

1. Become a "people-oriented" school. Expect teachers to teach so that children want to come to school every day. Genuine love and respect from teachers encourages children to develop more respect and love for themselves.
2. Provide freedom from threat—show consistent respect for each other.
3. Keep native curiosity alive and well—develop respect for natural thinking in each learner.
4. Teach youngsters to analyze their own thinking (metacognitive skills).
5. Develop—and emphasize—real, genuine communication; listen to children, and give them time to talk. Many self-directing ideas come out of a 3-minute dialogue with a child.
6. Show that knowledge is for use, not just for answering questions. (Before using SDL, the typical teacher asks

28 questions to each one a student asks; in SDL classrooms, this ratio is reversed.)

7. Develop high input for *personal* learning. Each student should identify some things he or she wants to
learn. Over time, expect precise identification of ways
they can learn those chosen items. If what we have
students do does not have much input into their lives,
what is its value? Disciplining, organizing, arranging,
and rule setting—all does little to help a student with
personal learning unless he or she has personal involvement in it.

8. Urge children to develop a personal code of ethics
they can live by. This requires dialogue about moral
standards, ethics, and values, which takes time. But
a personal code of ethics stays with a student for
a lifetime—so teachers must be given time for the
task.

9. Assist each student in developing a personal plan for
learning and one for self-discipline.

10. Enlist parents in SDL philosophy and identify the
kind of help they might give.

11. Expect each child to learn how to evaluate certain
aspects of his or her own work, whether it is subject
matter content, skills, psychological perspectives, or
keeping a "running tab" on how the child is learning
to control his or her own life.

If you choose to use self-directing philosophy and its
components in your school, you won't go back to old
methods—either students nor teachers would let you.
SDL gives students a "handle" on their inner selves, enabling them to reach new heights of achievement.

Effective Principals Are SDL Models

Henry A. Peel, Associate Professor
Department of Educational Leadership
East Carolina University
Greenville, North Carolina

To be an empowering principal, one must have

■ Strong commitment,
■ Willingness to take risks,
■ Willingness to communicate, and
■ Awareness of potential problems.

The concepts of SDL are both compatible with and essential to the responsibilities of on-the-job principals. If we want children to take responsibility for their own behavior, the principal must first encourage teachers to give them responsibility—plenty of it. Second, if we want children to become actively involved in deciding what kind of classroom or school they want, the principal must apply strategies that allow the children to create acceptable guidelines of conduct, allow for negotiation and creative decision making, and maximize student choice in setting goals. Third, SDL includes helping teachers learn they are to be "in control of helping students get in control"—a time-consuming responsibility that is more difficult than just telling students to follow some preset rules. Fourth, the principal who implements SDL philosophy must help teachers produce learning strategies of learning that can aid students in managing their own learning. Fifth, for successful implementation of SDL, teachers should be offered in-service workshops.

What higher-order self-directing behaviors does a principal need?

■ The ability to shift from controlling children to helping them control themselves;

- ■ Having a purpose in daily living and demonstrating this belief in contact with people;
- ■ A need for giving and receiving love—thinking about what is good for children; and
- ■ Internalizing the meaning of truth, goodness, aesthetic appreciation, ethical standards, and spiritual awakening—seeing all life as sacred and all human beings as of equal worth.

A strong part of the SDL program is its focus on helping students take charge of their own lives. The most noteworthy contribution the principal can make is to present a living example consciously using the same SDL behaviors.

The High/Scope Curriculum

Although our research has found no completely self-directing schools in the United States, several important facets of the SDL program have been used in the High/Scope Project at Perry Elementary School in Ypsilanti, Michigan, as a supplement to their regular educational programs.

The High/Scope curriculum is a framework of educational ideas and practices based on Piaget's theory of the natural development of young children. The High/Scope staff, headed by David P. Weikart, believes that children learn best from activities they themselves plan, carry out, and reflect on (Weikart & Schweinhart, 1993). The teachers join in those activities, asking questions that extend children's plans and help them think beyond the activity as they may have first envisioned it. The students make choices, solve problems, and engage in personally selected activities that contribute to their intellectual, social, and physical development.

An important aspect of the High/Scope Project is the role of the teacher interacting with the student. The teacher listens to what children plan, then works with them to extend their activities to more challenging levels. The teacher's questioning style is important, asking, "What happened?" "How did you make that?" "What do you know now that you didn't know a while ago?" This approach is different from the traditional roles of *active* teacher and *passive* students. Independent thinking is encouraged and self-directing activities enhance it. In both High/Scope and SDL, the programs emphasize helping students to make choices, solve problems, and generally engage in activities that promote social, intellectual, and physical development. A major difference is that SDL goes beyond academic acquisition, allowing students to assess and change their own perceptions for the purpose of changing their behaviors.

The High/Scope curriculum is used in thousands of early childhood programs throughout the United States. It received high acclaim from Alfie Kohn, author of *The Brighter Side of Human Nature: Altruism and Empathy in Everyday Life* (1990), who suggests that for youths to grow into caring adults, they must not only be taught by adults who care but must also have early school experiences that teach them to care about others. Researchers focused on a group of children in the experimental schools (then in kindergarten) and found that achievement differed significantly from that of their counterparts in the comparison schools.

Investigators of the High/Scope pilot program at the Perry School found that by the time these children reached sixth grade, they were outscoring their counterparts in the comparison schools in higher-order reading comprehension. Moreover, they were more likely to speak up in a discussion (self-directing behavior), even if their position seemed unlikely to prevail (Schweinhart et al., 1986, 1993).

A Study of Fifth Graders' Use of Self-Directing Perceptions and Learning Strategies

An 8-week study (Lane, 1992) was conducted of 152 fifth graders and their six teachers, using the Bradley-Lane Self-Directing Perceptual Scale, emphasizing self-directing behaviors and learning strategies. Two striking findings emerged. First, the experimental group of students (at all IQ levels) acquired more learning strategies than the control group, and second, most students nearly doubled their previous number of learning strategies. We concluded that children who are not taught learning strategies will probably never acquire the same repertoire of skills as students who are given this information.

Thus, learning strategies should be taught to all students, regardless of intellectual level. Rather than have students follow the traditional single strategy to learn a given subject, self-directed learners are encouraged to discover or invent newer and more creative strategies for their personalized learning and to achieve their goals.

4 Changing Student Perceptions

Traditional teaching causes students to lean on their teachers for cut-and-dried answers, but self-directed learning makes leaning unnecessary, even for students managing their own behavior.

Principals who wish to implement ideas about SDL often ask, "What do I tell my teachers to do?" This chapter helps answer that question.

We know that we are not just to *look* for well-behaved children, stars, and geniuses—we are to *develop* them. Likewise, if we look for self-directed learners, we may not turn up very many, but developing in young minds the necessary attributes and skills is definitely within our ability.

The wise person searches for meaning within his personal life and carefully weighs the influences that others have on it. The earlier a person finds out what guides his life, the more likely he will become a king of living, rather than a pawn. Children are no exception. They are guided by their inner thoughts, which come mostly from perceptions they acquire at an early age, typically modeled by the "significant others" closest to them.

Recognizing vividly the need for adults in society who are in charge of conduct and behavior, the Brock (n.d.) report, *An American Imperative: Higher Expectations for Higher Education,* seeks commitment from the nation's colleges to ensure "that next year's entering students will graduate as individuals of character, more sensitive to the needs of the community, more competent to contribute to society, and more civil in habits of thought, speech, and action" (pp. 1-3). But we believe such commitment and training must start much earlier than this, in early childhood with 4- and 5-year-olds, and must definitely be emphasized during the guidance of self-directing experiences of children from kindergarten through high school. It is our observation that even with limited instruction, some students can be provided with a personalized plan for the purpose of changing unfavorable behaviors to better ones.

Self-Understanding in Childhood and Adolescence

By age 11, a child ordinarily reaches a plateau of artistic maturity, but is likely to remain there throughout life unless given art training. Similarly, some children have limited understanding of how to control their emotions and actions, or how to get in charge of their lives. They may also stay at a low-level understanding of why they behave as they do, unless they receive sound instruction given from some simple, but concise, perspectives.

Every child is potentially a child psychologist. From a very early age, children acquire ideas, attitudes, and ethical information about themselves and others. These ideas may be healthy or not, true or false, satisfying or morbid. The child's development—mental, social, emotional, psychological, attitudinal, moral, and ethical—is too often left to chance.

Children's education should include principles of metacognitive dialogue and control theory principles, and different perspectives should be a planned feature of the education that children receive in elementary, middle, and secondary schooling. Some children will have persistent feelings of inferiority or other unhealthy attitudes regarding their personal worth. It is a bold measure to work with a child's perceptions, but preventing or solving problems is a better way to help youths than to wait until they are already mentally "on the rocks." When children study why people behave as they do, they seem fascinated with *self-understanding*. Knowledge of self is first perceived on an intellectual level, and from that point, youngsters will initiate further exploration themselves.

Texas teacher John Dawson found that children as young as fourth grade could understand the concept of SDL. Until then, many had not thought much about changing any behaviors.

A Practical Application

Accepting the premise that "learning to manage inward thoughts and emotions is just as an important part of school teaching as is teaching the facts and skills of the respective disciplines," fourth-grade teacher Dawson used his own ideas and several from Bradley and Lane's (1996) *Teacher Guidebook,* a booklet designed for professionals who use the student booklet, *A Personal Guide to My Own Thought Processes* (Areglado, Bradley, & Lane, in press). Each student was given his or her personal booklet for reading and for discussion purposes. Dawson found that its contents served the needs of intermediate-grade students and that its concepts could be refined down to the understanding and perceptual powers of his fourth graders. Some students openly expressed the value the authors' ideas had on their own lives. It was the first book of this type they had seen. As a forerunner to Dawson's other observations, it was a striking finding that a number of students had not, up to then, thought much about changing any behaviors, nor had they realized it was up to them to want to change. In student interviews, some revealed that they thought it was "up to the school to try to change them." Moreover, they really didn't know how to go about establishing the new behavior so it would become a workable part of their lives. It was also interesting to see the changes that took place when students tried their adjusted or new behaviors on various classmates and on their teacher. Additionally, the Bradley-Lane Self-Directing Perceptual Scale (Lane, 1996) was not only used for diagnostic purposes but, according to Dawson, became an excellent vehicle for guiding their seminar discussions as students sought more information on what to do to change behaviors they wished to eliminate or improve. Dawson knew his students well enough by April, when the perceptual scale was administered to his class, to discover how this assessment matched his own observations of student behavior, and he averred, "I was genuinely amazed and pleased to find the Bradley-Lane Self-Directing Perceptual Scale matched realistically my own observations of students and their overt behaviors, having watched and studied them over a period of time. Additionally, I was pleased to discover a few problems that were not picked up by personal observation and techniques, and these might have gone overlooked had the perceptual scale not been used." Dawson's field testing of the self-directing materials can be summarized in his comment: "Self-directed learning gives the student power thoughts for enabling one to reach one's true potential. The next step is personal commitment to action."

Encouraging and Nurturing Change

The Importance of Perceptions

The growing self must feel that it is involved—that it is really a part of what is going on and that in some degree, its involvement in thinking of all it takes in is helping to shape its own destiny. The acceptance of change through one's cognitive powers (thinking about those thoughts that seem to be the basis for guiding one's life) brings about modifications of behavior, personality, and emotions. One who accepts change in beliefs, concepts, and perceptions *behaves differently*. That person sees the pitfalls of a stoic, static personality that seeks to stop the process of creation, stifles the potential within, and hinders the goal of becoming a private, unique self-fulfilled individual. Life to the fully functioning individual is one of discovery and adventure.

Behavior Is Determined by a Person's Perceptions

Individuals react to stimuli in terms of their perceptions of them, what those stimuli appear to be, what they mean to their internal assessment. "We see things," says a perceptual psychologist, "not as *they* are but as *we* are" (Gibson, 1951, pp. 85-110). The phrase should not be "seeing is believing," but "believing is seeing." Beliefs, attitudes, expectations, and desires influence students' perceptions and thus their behavior.

This theory of behavior helps us to understand more clearly both the reasonable and unreasonable behavior of others. To illustrate, take the case of the teenage motorcyclist who stops at a stop sign, then immediately proceeds left into the path of an oncoming vehicle. "That motorcyclist must be blind," thinks the driver behind him. (The driver of the car that nearly hit the teenager will no doubt have a less charitable reaction.) The teenager's action seems negligent, but if you recognize that he perceived the intersection as a four-way stop, such behavior is understandable, even though it nearly caused him to get hit.

Self-Directed Learning Cultivates
Strong, Positive Feelings About Self

The self is the center around which all of an individual's other perceptions are organized. A person who perceives himself as one who can't get along with others, won't. Holding this conviction, he doesn't try, so of course he fails. Unless he acquires pictures in his mind that he can cope, that he can learn how to behave better toward others, it is useless to just make him behave in the right ways, because that is external control, not personal control. When the outside control is taken away, he performs as he always has.

If behavior is determined by one's perceptions, then to understand and predict another's behavior, one must know that person's internal and external frames of reference. Great teachers are those who can place themselves in the learner's shoes. The teacher must become skilled in how to take an *internal* rather than the usual *external* frame of reference if he is going to understand, help, and change students' essential behaviors. Atticus Finch, the lawyer in *To Kill a Mockingbird,* in trying to help his children understand the behavior of others, says, "You never really understand a person until you consider things from his point of view—until you climb into his skin and walk around in it" (Lee, 1960, p. 36). Those who truly wish to change children's perceptions must develop a respect for them, be genuine with them, and cultivate their own empathy more completely while nurturing each student's perceptual changes.

A teacher must ask a student to reveal her perceptions of a demonstrated behavior before he (and perhaps the child) can understand why she behaved as she did. If you want to change a child's perceptions, you must help her acquire behaviors that will let her perceive positive thoughts. To change an attitude, the student must first produce the behavior she wants, practice that behavior, and then the attitude will come gradually. In essence, she grows into the attitudinal change. Likewise, if you explain clearly to a youngster the perception she must hold to acquire a certain behavior, practicing that behavior ultimately helps her acquire the perception necessary to make it an automatic part of her life.

To Change Behavior, We Must
Also Change the Perception

Because perceptions, particularly of self, determine behavior, it becomes clear that a student must change perceptions to change behavior. A student is usually willing to change perceptions in situations that are not working, and with some encouragement from the teacher, to work on those situations. This may be why much of what children are exposed to in school has little, if any, effect—they don't see it as relevant. So a major condition for perceptual change is an experience that has personal meaning. The insightful teacher will help each child match perceptions and accompanying behaviors. Perceptual change does not often occur when an individual feels threatened, so the experience that leads to change must raise a provocative question or a striking problem for the student to analyze in a challenging, rather than a threatening, way. When a child feels threatened or coerced, he does not accept the idea as his own and tends to tense up and defend himself.

Self-Directing Principles for Students

The most successful teachers and principals are those who have the skill to see what students see, think what they think, and feel what they feel. Unless adults master this ability, they will continue to react in a harmful or nonhelpful manner and will probably not try to help a student until he poses a threat or problem. Then the emphasis is usually on *corrective* measures, in which the offender is reminded of rules, controlled by penalties, or isolated in some way from the classroom. More often than not, he is turned over to the principal.

The program of self-control and management offered in this book, however, is preventive. *Before* a student gets into trouble, she is given instruction about how to control her behaviors. She is asked to be introspective—to look inside her own mind to see the thoughts on which she has based past reactions—to self, school, teachers, friends, and parents. Her teacher gives her examples of the types of thoughts it takes to get and stay in charge of her actions. She is encouraged to practice by thinking these new thoughts over and over. Just as a golf player practices putting, then plugs it back into his total game plan, the student practices thoughts that will help her control her next reaction, then plugs these new ways of thinking back into her plan of self-discipline.

The skills for being in charge of one's life are learned skills—they do not come naturally. We have to work at obtaining, using, and refining these skills. As we advocated these principles for widespread use, we had them field-tested to see how they worked. Samples of self-directing principles shared with a fourth-grade class are listed in Figure 4.1 (samples of perceptions for a first-grade class are in Resource C).

These 20 perceptions are not intended to elicit a parroting response, where students repeat what they think adults want to hear. Rather, they are a guide for teachers' questions about what might lie hidden in student responses, and what risks are necessary to gain tighter control over personal thoughts and behaviors. These principles are only representative and not inclusive.

1. My feelings come from my thoughts. Therefore, if I want to be in charge of my life, I must teach myself to think thoughts that will bring out the best feelings and behaviors.
2. I am responsible for every act I do. I won't say, "They made me do it!" or "It's not my fault." I will say, "I did it," and "I will assume the responsibility for it."
3. To stay in control of my life, *I will have a plan.* For example, I will treat others the way I want them to treat me. If someone hits me, I will hit back only if it's necessary to defend myself. I won't knowingly go where trouble is. If someone yells at me, I won't yell back, but I'll still be in control, because I've learned that if I use a soft voice, the "yeller" will lower his voice, too. I will stop letting little things irritate me—like dropping pencils, or someone knocking things off my desk.
4. I must make my body do the right thing, rather than just let it do what it wants. If I have power over myself, I can control my diet, motivation, muscle tone, rest, and play, because these are personal things. I will devise a workable plan to do this. For example, if I disobey my parents and watch TV late on a school night, I won't allow myself to be grumpy the next day.
5. Learning to manage my inward thoughts and emotions is just as important to my school program as learning the facts and skills of the subjects I study.
6. As a thinking person, I don't always need the approval of others to feel good about myself. Everybody needs friends, but not "friends" who make you do things that get you into trouble. The stronger I am as a person, the more I can choose my own friends. Although approval by those I like is nice, I don't have to join a gang to feel good about myself. In fact, the more I look within myself to determine what is right, the more I increase my chances of obtaining approval from others, anyway.
7. I can help others better after first learning to live with love, fairness, and ethical behavior myself. If I live joyously myself, then my words and actions match each other. This alone sends a vivid message. Classmates are not people to compete with but people I can help to do their best.

Figure 4.1. Twenty Perceptions for Students

8. The more power I hold over myself, to control myself and exercise self-discipline, the less power I will feel I need. Instead of trying to make *others* do what I want them to, I will make *myself* do what I need to. I may not be able to control what happens to me, but if I choose, I can always control how I react to what happens.

9. If I want things to happen in my life, I must be willing to do things to make them happen. There is no need for someone to prod me. I must simply make myself do what I ought to.

10. I become what I think about. I must hold exciting pictures in my head of what I want to be and do. Dreams won't come true for people who don't have dreams.

11. I need to practice visual imagery. If I picture myself giving a good oral report and practice how to do it in my head, it will help me do a good job when I'm in front of the class.

12. I will not put myself down—for any reason. There is harm in telling myself, "I'm no good!" or "No one likes me." What I need is to do something good for somebody, then feel good about myself for doing it.

13. If I'm depressed, perhaps because I did poorly on my last test, I should forget about it and instead do something constructive to keep from doing a bad job next time.

14. If I want to change a current behavior, I must practice the new behavior I want for 21 days or more. The attitude I want will then come naturally. Any change in attitude requires me to practice the behavior first, then the attitude will take over.

15. I can change anything about myself if I set my mind to it. No one can change me; it is up to me to change myself.

16. Some of my responses to things, people, and myself have become automatic. I need to look at these automatic responses and see if any of my actions are inappropriate now. Those that are should be kicked out of my mind, new ones chosen to replace them, and those new ones practiced.

17. Instead of allowing myself to be bored, I will think thoughts and do things that remove boredom from my life. Life is too exciting to be bored with it!

18. I must be truthful to myself—face my strengths and weaknesses squarely. For example, "My low grade in spelling is because I didn't study, not because the teacher doesn't like me."

19. My happiness doesn't depend on what others do; it depends on what I do. It's my own actions that make me happy.

20. Words that others say about me will hurt me only if I let them. I may find, on assessment, that I don't like the words because they're true. So if I change my behavior, that person cannot truthfully say that about me again. I will know I did all I could to change—it's my choice!

Figure 4.1. Continued

Self-Concept and Behavior

A child's self-concept is made up of the perceptions and con-
victions she has about herself. The self-concept is developmental
because it is influenced by the past and by anticipated experiences
of the future. The cues received from significant others, including
teachers, are very influential in forming a child's self-concept.

Belonging Is a Basic Need

A child's basic need to belong is reflected in her self-concept,
and teachers have opportunities to affect the way a student meets
that need through caring relationships. The teacher should help
a student identify ways she can become responsible for her actions
and be recognized for her contributions, thereby enhancing her
self-concept. With diligence and compassion, a teacher can often
move a child's view from "I can't do it" to "I'll get it done."

Cues from the significant people in a child's life can negatively
influence his self-concept. Because behavior is a reflection of a
person's self-concept, undesirable behavior is a probable outcome
of low self-esteem. If most of the cues a child receives are anger,
annoyance, ridicule, rejection, distrust, or impatience, a child
develops a feeling of failure and low self-esteem. And that will
probably reflect itself in negative behavior—aggression, indif-
ference, failure, withdrawal, tension, hostility, fear, guilt, or sub-
missiveness.

By contrast, positive cues—like acceptance, love, concern,
encouragement, security, empathy, sensitivity, and understanding—can give a sense of personal worth, which is reflected
in positive behavior and performance—success, creativity,
achievement, interest, identification, cooperation, curiosity, and
enthusiasm (Weiking, 1969).

Students' Writing Can Sometimes
Tell What You Cannot See

Another technique for gaining insight into a child's perceptions and self-concept is to use creative writing and unfinished

sentences, where the teacher controls only the topics. The answers to unfinished sentences like these may be revealing:

"I'm happy when . . ."
"School makes me feel . . ."
"I worry when . . ."
"I'd like to be . . ."
"Other people think I'm . . ."

Creative writing can help teachers learn more about the subject a child knows best—himself! Topics like the following may help a teacher understand the perceptions from which a child draws conclusions about himself: "If I had three wishes," "My biggest problem," "When I grow up," and "If I were the teacher." Such writing exercises also give the child the feeling that his teacher cares about him and his problems.

Video Cameras Tell a Lot

The use of videotape can be invaluable in establishing awareness of children's feelings and behavior. By placing in the classroom an unobtrusive camera focused on the children, the teacher can turn it on at her discretion and capture the classroom climate, facial expressions, and actions of individual children: discouragement, joy, boredom, frustration, pride, or disappointment. This procedure gives concrete evidence for analyzing the meanings of behavior and for searching for ways to help children with negative self-concepts or other problems.

Once the teacher feels confident in her identification of the perceptions a youngster holds, she can formulate a plan with his assistance. If, for instance, he has been "acting out" to get attention, with the teacher's help he works on a plan to complete some successful production that he can show to the entire class. The teacher can then genuinely praise him for his contribution, thus rewarding the student in the right way for the recognition he was seeking in the first place. In the future, with just limited encouragement, this student will seek something positive to do for similar recognition. He will *self-direct* in a more positive way.

Telling Students About Self-Directed Learning

Students need to hear as much as they can about SDL—it is to them that self-directing principles and expectations are to be applied. They may ask, "Why should I become more responsible for my own learning?" Below are samples of what to tell them. Choose your own way of saying it, but explain carefully what SDL is all about.

When a baby is born it's totally dependent on its parents—they must feed it, carry it, make decisions for it. But as the baby gets older, it has an increasing psychological need to be independent. It doesn't want teachers or parents making all of its decisions. And the further the child goes in school, he or she becomes psychologically knowledgeable enough to be more independent. An essential aspect of growing up is developing the ability to take increasing responsibility for our own lives. It doesn't happen overnight—we *learn,* with the help of parents, teachers, and others—how to take more effective control of our lives, to become step-by-step increasingly self-directing.

Schools and classrooms are being restructured. Such developments (nongraded schools and classrooms, outcome-based education, magnet schools, independent study, and contract learning) put much responsibility for learning on students' shoulders. To be ready for this new trend, you must begin now to take more initiative for your own learning.

Over a long period of time, you have put in your mind pictures (perceptions), which are the basis for telling yourself what you can or cannot do. You got these perceptions by reading them, hearing about them, or watching others. But they are there! Some are good, strong pictures, but some are fuzzy, and not very good to hold any longer. Because you put the pictures in your mind, you can take them out. No one else can do this for you. So it's your choice as you start to analyze yourself. If a perception isn't working, or if you find a better image, you can replace an old one.

Suppose someone told you, "You can't learn. You never will! You're a dummy!" Pretend that at that time you believed it. So you began telling yourself repeatedly, "I can't learn. I never will. I'm a dummy!" If you really did this for several months, it's possible that your perception of yourself and your capability were distorted. Because you reinforced that negative, erroneous belief, you unwittingly programmed yourself for failure and a bad self-image. You may have gone to bed as a nonlearner (in your thoughts), looked in the mirror in the morning and saw a poor learner, and brushed the teeth of a dummy. Then, all of a sudden, you thought you really were a dummy.

Someone criticizes us, scares us, or calls us names—and we get the wrong picture. And if our mind stores that picture, we tend to become like that picture. But you can rid yourself of that image the same way you acquired it. Tell yourself you can learn! Learn something within the next 48 hours to prove it. Have your mind tell yourself you can be successful, and over a period of time, with practice, you can be a winner! Go to bed thinking of yourself as a learner. Get up a winner. Look in the mirror each morning and praise the genius looking back at you. Smile, and thank yourself for being a great learner. Brush the teeth of a genius; pick up your lunch money and head for school with a big smile on your face.

Back to reality, you say? But you remain a genius. Take any bad pictures out of your mind and put in the new perceptions of yourself as a *new* you—the good learner! Study and practice what it takes to make this new you, and you will become more successful. It's all up to you.

Most of you don't have to worry about this example because you're good learners already. But maybe you can be a better learner than you now are. You can become self-directed learners if you choose. Each of us must get in charge of his or her perceptions and actions. If we don't control ourselves through our thinking, someone else will.

Help Children Think Things Through

Don't tell students what to do. Instead, see that they have the right information to tell themselves what to do (see Figure 4.2). In the Japanese culture, if a child is running around in the grocery store, a parent might say, "How do you think the manager feels when you're tearing around, bumping into customers and knocking things over?" The child has to think through his answer. In U.S. schools, we say to a misbehaving child, "Do you want to stay after school? Do you want to fail?" Why don't we say, "Others are trying to work right now; why don't you help them out?" The point is, when a student is put into a position that requires a self-directing response, one that makes him think it through and arrive at his own decision, he is more ready for the consequences, positive or negative. The responsibility for action is on his shoulders, not the school's.

Help Students Avoid Pressure

Teach children that stress comes from the way they think, not from people around them or situations over which they have no control. Don't give them excuses to feel stressed: "You're going to have a test on this material Friday, so you'd better listen today." Instead, say, "Can you identify the meaning behind this material so you can apply it the next time you encounter it?" Suggest, "Here's three positive things you can do to withstand the pressure you are feeling at the moment." When you see a student occupied with stress, see if you can help her push the thought away for 60 seconds. Each time it begins to invade her consciousness, teach her to push it away and refuse to think that thought for 1 minute. This may sound simplistic, but it is the basis for eliminating

You learn from everything you do; you could just sit and listen to the teacher and learn. But today you must do more. There is so much new information, and some of it goes out-of-date so quickly, you have to develop skills to learn on your own so you can go on learning easily for the rest of your life.

You need to acquire understanding of how to deal with changing ideas and new information that bombard us every day via the computer, news media, and television. This rapidly changing world affects your thinking and how you perceive yourself in it. You have a responsibility to develop some basic standards to live by, that you can build on in the future. You must study how you perceive things, which means trying to analyze your perceptions (e.g., "If I think this, what actions will it likely cause me to take?"). Most of our actions are a result of the way we see things in our minds.

From your own consciousness, you can draw some ideas on how to do the following:

■ Diagnose your own needs (make rating scales, plot spelling graphs, look at what you missed on a test).

■ Formulate some personal living goals (identify statements that show your ethical viewpoints, assess your mental pictures about the joy of living).

■ Identify human and material resources you can use to find out information (Mr. Jones knows a lot about plants and trees; true stories about people appear in *Reader's Digest*).

■ Choose learning strategies to use on an assignment, then regularly add new ones to your list of ways to learn.

■ Evaluate your own learning outcomes in some systematic ways.

■ Use what you're learning today in some real-world experiences. You will discover a connection between what you learn and how you learn it. You'll feel smarter and better prepared for today's work than you were yesterday. Each day it will become easier to learn. You will feel your own accumulation of learning power. *Self-directed learning can be fun!*

Figure 4.2. Why Should I Be a Self-Directing Learner?

self-defeating thoughts—with practice! Rather than sit and be stressed out, urge the student to do something positive, even if it means changing locations for just a few minutes. This shows she is still in control, that excess stress is not controlling her.

You might discuss the following scenarios with students:

■ If you genuinely disagree with someone, don't always alter your behavior just because they show signs of disapproval.

■ Don't go along with the crowd when you think what they're doing is wrong.

■ Don't say, "This is just the way I am; I can't do anything about it." You can change anything about your life if you really choose to do so.

■ Talk about what to say when someone suggests doing the wrong thing: "You feel I should steal the baseball from the 7-Eleven store, just to help *you* have a good time?" It helps the student to realize these are not his own feelings, but what the other person wants him to do. If he thinks twice about it, he might not choose to do it at all.

Develop a Workable Plan—And Stick to It!

It pays to think through what one is going to do throughout life. A plan need not be set in concrete, but can be modified and changed as the need arises. The following guidelines can assist you in the beginning—they need not be followed blindly. When you have to decide if something is right or wrong for you, apply these tests:

Common sense. Is it reasonable? Will it be helpful in getting what I need right now? Will what I do seriously affect my life, and for the right reasons?

Giving your best shot. Are you giving what you choose to do your best shot?

Sportsmanship. When one player violates the rules, the whole team is penalized. Will what you do hurt others?

The hero test. Would you like the hero you believe in to know what you are doing? What might that hero say? Who would be most proud or most hurt by your decision? Would you want your hero to model him- or herself after you?

Publicity. Suppose what you are choosing to do would be shown on TV for the world to see—would you be willing to publicize your actions?

Foresight. Be sure the road you choose is the one that will take you where you want to go. Who else may have taken this path already? How did they fare? What obstacles might you encounter? How will you handle them? If all goes well, what might your life be like in a year? 2 years? 5 years?

Avoiding Pitfalls

One of the most common pitfalls a teacher can fall into is to allow students to get by without a plan of action. Most of the time, conventional teachers tell students what to do. If students do not have goals, teachers tend to set school goals for them, even if they are contrived and superficial. Until students are able to set their own goals, it is still better to supply them each with some tentative possibilities and have them negotiate the extent to which these goals will be achieved. If students have trouble setting goals, they will probably also have trouble reaching them without a lot of teacher encouragement. Teachers should check progress intermittently and provide encouragement along the way. It should then be only a short time until students are able to cite and set some personal goals.

Establishing a definite agenda and setting goals for planning ahead, although these may be somewhat informal, prevent a sense of hopeless drifting. When students direct their own activities, they need to feel that they are making measurable progress. Otherwise, discouragement is likely to set in. SDL teachers watch for any indication that the student has begun to doubt, falter, or lose sight of personal goals.

Another pitfall to avoid, because students do a lot on their own, is failing to evaluate a student's work. Teachers should simply tell a student how he is doing every once in a while, going over his portfolio or having a jury of peers look at the work. Both procedures are effective.

Teachers today can still make a real difference in the lives of students. Knowledge is ever changing, but well-grounded perceptions (even the wrong ones) follow most people for most of their lives. So when students study perceptions and identify the thoughts one needs as guidelines, then they have acquired intellectual and psychological skills they can use for a lifetime. It would be wise if all of us would cultivate perceptions that we have tested, and continuously refine them. They become the foundation for the plan against which all the future behaviors of our lives are evaluated.

Actions are based on one's previous perceptions. When you describe a person, you tell about her behavior. A person's overt behavior tells who and what she is. Therefore, to change behaviors, one must make one's thoughts and actions congruent. The well-informed SDL teacher will assist children in thinking about themselves, but should not be expected to go it alone in helping students formulate better perceptions.

The school principal must offer more leadership in the area of children's perceptual development. A first step is encouraging teachers to produce more formal lessons on "thinking about thinking." Educators must set out to help students realize that the key to success is the one that unlocks the knowledge and beliefs in their own minds. William Blake was right: "Man's desires are limited by his *perceptions*; none can desire what he has not perceived."

Directing one's own thoughts or feelings requires a lot of personal psychological strength. And it takes a lot of self-directing for a student—or anyone else—to change a psychological behavior. But to know that you are in control of your own thoughts brings a lot of joy to life. The serendipitous effect is equally significant: The more self-directing people are, the more responsibility they assume for working on moral and ethical problems in society. One reason might be that those who are able to successfully manage their own lives feel more enabled to reach out, take risks, and give time to things beyond themselves. They know they can make a difference.

Self-Directing Behavior Becomes Self-Discipline

Schools use a number of management programs designed to "make" students behave or "pay the price" if they do not. Only a few of these programs offer guidance on how youths can manage their own emotions and behaviors in a *conscious* manner. The self-discipline program described in this book (see also Bradley, 1991, 1992), puts students immediately in charge of their own behavior—learners are taught what they must know and must do to be fully in charge of personal behavior.

Self-directing teachers seek to teach youngsters that they must learn to do more of what they *should* than to allow themselves to do only what they *want*. With a little practice, a lot of patience, and commitment to the principles outlined here, a willing teacher can confer with a student on a regular basis and negotiate behaviors that make a difference in a child's life, rather than just the momentary needs of the classroom or school. There is an amazing change in most students who develop a personalized behavior plan under the auspices of a teacher who is well versed in self-direction. Students who can see that some reasonable concepts will change their lives are usually willing to commit time and effort to achieving these goals. The personal plan of self-control becomes a commitment to self, and they realize that the teacher's expertise will help them prevent problems in their own lives. Most students can be taught how to manage their own thinking much better than they now do, and when they start to control their thinking they also assume more responsibility for their subsequent behavior.

What would one expect to see a self-directing teacher demonstrate in assisting a student to develop a personalized plan of self-discipline? The teacher

1. Continually helps the student to develop and maintain control over what he does;
2. Treats an individual with respect, even though she may deviate from the chosen plan from time to time;
3. Holds each student responsible for his acts;

4. Doesn't wait for things to get better, but plans ahead so things will improve;

5. Believes that learning to manage one's inward thoughts and emotions is just an important part of schooling as the teaching of facts and skills in the curriculum;

6. Recognizes that before you can change others, you have to first be willing to change yourself; and

7. Encourages youths to plan for great things in their lives. Children who feel they can be winners do more of the right things academically, and demonstrate better behavior.

Dealing With Student Anger

Look around you. An alarming amount of anger is being demonstrated, by all kinds of people. We do not want our children to grow up with anger and hatred in their hearts, to have continual outbursts that go unchecked. Behavior that reflects anger, and that continues unchecked into adulthood without any attempt to control it, will become as detrimental to the perpetrator as to the victim.

What Is Anger?

Anger often shows itself through yelling, fussing, striking out verbally or physically, or throwing tantrums. Children learn at a very early age that an expression of anger usually brings them an immediate, desired result. Some children carry the same behaviors into school—throwing a tantrum in the grocery store because Mother won't buy the gum they want, crying until they get to go play with the neighbor, or hitting. Even adults try to cover angry outbursts that get them into trouble by saying, "I have a quick temper—I can't help myself." These are cop-outs—anger *is* a result of thinking. These people are using anger to get their way because they do not try to control their behavior.

What to Do

First, do not be afraid to confront student's angry outbursts. Make it clear to the class that anger will not be the way in which they relate to you or their classmates to get what they want. Remember that if you give in to anger, rage, tantrums, or irrational arguing, you could be encouraging students to use these strategies throughout life. Avoid thinking, "He can't help how he acts—look at his home life," or "She just threw another tantrum—well, it's only human nature." All of these excuses must go if we wish to help a child be rational instead of irrational.

Anger and its outbursts do not come from other people or things in the world—it comes from how a person *views* the world from inside his or her own mind. This is important to teach your students. It may be more easily understood this way: "Our feelings come from our thoughts. If we control our thoughts, we can control our feelings. Thoughts of anger come from our own minds. If we can control those thoughts, we can control our behaviors." *Angry thoughts create angry reactions.*

To the first grader who throws a Lincoln log because he can't find the one that he needs, the teacher should say, "I see you are thinking angry thoughts, but do they help you find the missing log? It isn't the missing log that made you upset—it was the angry thoughts. Why don't you try waiting a few seconds the next time you think you're going to get angry, and in those few seconds look more carefully for the missing piece? Don't let your thoughts keep you from getting the best out of yourself." It may take several occasions for the student to fully realize what he has to do to get in charge of his angry thoughts, but don't let him offer excuses for his unruly behavior—"I was just letting off steam!" If a child is going to control his behavior, he must learn that he will do it consciously with his brain.

Of course, children will have angry thoughts and will need to give vent to their feelings, but we must teach them that hitting "Bozo the Clown," kicking the soccer ball, or going off by oneself for a few minutes are better ways of handling angry thoughts

than screaming, hitting, swearing, or anything else that is directly aimed at another person. Moreover, we need to make it clear
that we will not allow such behavior directed at another for any
reason. Accepting a child's expression of anger in a way that is not
harmful to others is healthier than letting him store it away for a
later psychological explosion.

Perhaps the greatest way of helping a child handle angry
moods is to help him direct the anger consciously toward thoughts
that will help him change a behavior, rather than ignore it. Failing
to face up to a behavior can immobilize a person and keep him
from getting what he wants.

The Self-Directed Plan of Discipline

Discipline in school can take on a new meaning if we are
willing to work at it. Discipline can become a *learning* experience,
rather than punishment, but it will take a new approach to change
most people's concept of the word (see Figure 4.3). *Discipline
should bring inner rewards rather than outer punishments.* The
personalized discipline plan is a written plan negotiated between the teacher and the student. The ideas it contains are
commensurate with a child's maturational development, ability
to understand and comprehend, and physical age.

Figure 4.4 illustrates the types of personal messages to give
intermediate grade levels through personal and group conversing
techniques.

After approximately 10 meetings of 15-minutes each in which
all students in a group are made aware of the perceptions to hold
if they wish to get in charge of themselves, Figure 4.5 is given to
the students to assess where they are in the whole process. It only
takes a few minutes to itemize the responses or to simply peruse
them as a group to see what needs further explanation in small
groups organized for similar needs.

Figure 4.6 illustrates a sample of what a given student might
learn from the lectures as the principles he thinks he should know
and start with for his own personalized, self-discipline plan.

(Text continues on p. 72.)

Anytown Elementary School
1111 Fairlawn Street
Anytown, Texas

April 15, 1996

Dear Parents:

To guarantee your child, and all our students, the excellent learning climate
they deserve, we will be using "The Self-Directed Plan of Discipline" that goes
into effect today (see attached). This is the plan that was discussed by our
PTO and explained during our recent Open House.

Our Philosophy: We believe that all students can and should behave appropriately in the classroom. We will not tolerate any student stopping us
from teaching, or their peers from learning.

The rules that my class and I have agreed on are simple and concise, but each
serves to nurture a child's growth and development. Our realistic goal is to
use discipline as a way to promote high-level personal values and cooperative
behavior in children, rather than simply as a way to maintain control in the
classroom. It is my intention that each student will soon learn to *internalize*
the standards and expectations I would like them to become committed to—to
adopt being self-controlled as their personal goal.

I wish to teach so students understand that people should hold themselves
responsible for their own actions. I will teach that each student must recognize that he is responsible for any acts he chooses to commit. Your child will
learn that everything we think and do comes from our thoughts. No one
causes us to do anything, so we can't blame others for our chosen actions. If
a child can learn how to control how she thinks, she can control how she acts.
This will be a new learning experience for some students. But I know that
with your help and your child's efforts, our students will become more in
charge of their own behavior.

Our agreed-on rules are very clear: not to harm others or ourselves; to
maintain values that respect the rights and dignity of others; to listen
courteously to their ideas; to show respect for school property; to exercise good
behavior everywhere in the school; to use proper language; to do assigned
work within a reasonable time and with pride; to maintain good attendance;
and to solve all problems encountered in a cooperative, systematic, and civil
manner. When there appears to be a conflict, both teacher and student
(including parents, if need be) will negotiate for a better behavior.

I wholeheartedly believe that the attached Self-Discipline Plan will assist
each child to consciously exercise more control over his own actions. Students
will be pleased once they demonstrate some effective controls (perceptions,
skills, behaviors) in their own lives.

Respectfully yours,
Ms. Jane Jensen
Fifth grade teacher

Figure 4.3. Sample Letter Informing Parents
NOTE: This letter would have been sent home with the student along with classroom rules
and self-discipline concepts.
SOURCE: Full acknowledgment and publishing credit given to *The TEPSA Journal* (Fall
1992), No. 46: 24-27 and 34, for an earlier treatise by coauthor Bradley on the same subject.

Conversing With Children

1. Bobby, if you write "I hate you," on your papers, you're just going to make a lot of people angry; most will send you to the principal. Why don't you get in charge of your life and stop choosing to do things that get you into trouble? Let's try to find some things in class you like, or let's come up with some new things for you that you will like. Then you can write, "I like this lesson" on your papers.

2. Sue! I see you as a movie star in a white satin dress, envied by the world, so I really don't understand why you keep putting yourself down and say that nobody likes you. Keep your hair fixed, look pretty, and keep a good attitude—discipline yourself to take care of yourself, and you'll be well liked.

3. No wonder Jimmy gets to go so many places by himself—he's always so well behaved and in charge of his behaviors.

4. I heard a person say today, "I'm sorry!" instead of "Now look what you made me do!" What kind of person do you think I met?

5. Every time I think I'm going to anger, I think more pleasant thoughts. Sometimes when someone is causing me to anger, I say to myself, "I'll try to put off angering at them for 10 seconds"—if I can do that, I can soon make it to 25 or 30 seconds, and then I may not have angering feelings at all because I am *controlling* them.

6. If I hold a picture long enough in my head as to what I want to be like, I will be able to find things to help me reach what I want to be. But I must practice the behaviors that I want, just like a golfer works on his putting game. I must work at it to become skilled. Working with people takes "people skills."

7. As a person, I do what others want, if it seems best, until I can prove to them that I have something that will better fulfill my skills or needs.

8. Angering is a habit. As I grow older, I won't grow out of the habit of angering unless I do something that helps me not to anger. Angry thoughts cause angry reactions!

9. Tell children, "I'm willing to *reason* with you to get what you want, but I will not allow you to express anger as your major way of obtaining it."

10. Put on a placard for your room: "In our room, we each have a plan for *self-discipline!* Ask someone here about it."

11. Repeatedly ask children who get into trouble: "Where did your plan go wrong? Was this difficulty something you had not yet taken care of in your plan? What is your plan now? Can I help you with your plan? What do you need to practice more? Will you follow a workable plan if I help you devise it? Why don't we negotiate for a better behavior (I will change some of my expectations if you will change to some more positive types of actions and behaviors. Fair enough?"

12. If you do not exercise control over yourself, then I will have to impose stronger controls of my own over you because I am to see that students in my class behave. Both our jobs are easier when you demonstrate the willingness and expertise to stay in control of your own life.

Figure 4.4. Example of a Self-Directed Plan of Discipline

SOURCE: Full acknowledgment and publishing credit given to *The TEPSA Journal* (Fall 1992), No. 46: 24-27 and 34, for an earlier treatise by coauthor Bradley on the same subject.

How many of the ideas below are a part of my own, personalized discipline plan?	I need help	I understand
1. Good behavior is practiced; it doesn't just come naturally for most people	___	___
2. How I react to things is a result of how I think inside myself; my reactions are not caused by other people.	___	___
3. Almost always, I can change what I do if I just think about it.	___	___
4. I will set some goals of behavior that I know I can master; I will practice these each day.	___	___
5. If I get in charge of myself and control my actions, I will not knowingly break any school rules.	___	___
6. I need to practice some "in control" time each day.	___	___
7. If I will seize control over the pictures in my head of what I want myself to be, I can become master of my own destiny.	___	___
8. No matter how I feel, if I will just think about what to do if someone angers me, I can think thoughts that will control my behaviors.	___	___
9. I can think what is the difference between good behavior and bad behavior. I have a good self to draw on for good results. I just have to choose to do it.	___	___
10. The more often I think about having a good attitude, the more often I will have a good day.	___	___
11. What I see (perceive) in my mind as my behavior is how I behave in the *outside* world (outside my mind).	___	___
12. Unless I choose to change what I do or how I think, I will not ever change what I feel, because if something bad happens to me, it will just seem natural to feel bad.	___	___
13. I am at my best when I teach myself to decide what behavior I want or need to use in some situation. I decide what steps to take to get that behavior and I then *do* that behavior.	___	___
14. I change whatever behavior that I have that feels bad for me.	___	___
15. The best way to keep my good behavior is to look closely at it each day and to correct small errors as soon as I notice I let them occur.	___	___
16. I have a "good self" because I know I can be good if I choose. From time to time, I need to remind myself I am good and to smile about it.	___	___

Figure 4.5. Getting Ready for Self-Discipline

How many of the ideas below are a part *of my own, personalized discipline plan?*	*I* *need help*	*I* *understand*
17. I have some angry thought patterns of behavior in my brain that are now automatic; I need to look at these behaviors and rethink some of them.	____	____
18. If I have some old automatic behaviors that I wish to get rid of and substitute a new behavior, I must practice the new behavior for 21 days before it will become automatic in my life.	____	____
19. I have the power to add a new behavior (perception) to my life if I want.	____	____
20. I should take at least one minute a day to review the extent to which my chosen behaviors and goals were carried out yesterday.	____	____
21. The way I treat others should be the way I want to be treated myself.	____	____
22. I must give more love away than hate. I must cause more joy in lives than sorrow. I must take a few more harsh words from others without fighting back. I can do this because others may not have a self-discipline plan in their minds. I can be a good model for them to witness.	____	____
23. When I start to break my self-discipline plan, I must rethink my commitment (promise) to myself. I must be honest with myself and make myself do what my mind tells me to do.	____	____
24. My feelings come from my thoughts. If I can control how and what I think, I can control my outward behavior toward others.	____	____
25. The next time someone irritates me or angers me, I will put off (restrain) any angering behaviors for 5 seconds. I will practice until I can count to 10 seconds, then 60 seconds. Someday, I won't have any angering feelings because I have been controlling them.	____	____
26. If I can demonstrate to others that I have control over myself, then I will have fewer people trying to control me.	____	____
27. Controlling myself (my behavior) at school is just as important a part of my school life as is learning the subject matter my teacher teaches.	____	____
28. Every time I'm about to get upset, I must choose more pleasant thoughts.	____	____
29. If I cannot get a good self-discipline plan for myself, then others will control me.	____	____
30. I must assume responsibility for every act I do.	____	____

Figure 4.5. Continued

SOURCE: Full acknowledgment and publishing credit given to *The TEPSA Journal* (Fall 1992), No. 46: 24-27 and 34, for an earlier treatise by coauthor Bradley on the same subject.

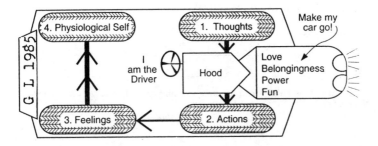

My special sports car is a front-end drive. I'm behind the wheel, guiding my own life. My *thoughts* (1) cause *actions,* (2) and from my actions I get (3) *feelings,* and all of this results in (4) changing my physical self. Therefore, if I control my thoughts, I can control my actions, and the actions I perform will bring forth the feelings I want. Because I believe this, I am responsible for every act I perform. And I can consciously bring forth any feeling behaviors I want by thinking the right thoughts.

Principles about thinking that I should understand

- My feelings come from my thoughts; if I can control my thoughts, I can control my feelings.
- If I believe in myself, I don't have to look to others to see who I am. I can learn to trust my own opinions about myself.
- It takes 21 (or more) days for most people to change their behaviors. Therefore, whatever I want to develop as a new behavior, I will have to practice each day until it becomes automatic.
- I should take at least one minute of my day to review the extent to which my chosen behavior goals have been carried out. If I then discover I've failed to exercise one or more of them, at that point, I must decide what I'm going to do to practice these chosen behavior goals further.
- If I continue to look for good in myself, I will see more good in others too. When I see good in others, I will praise them for it. I will thank them for being nice to me. And I will demonstrate nice behavior back to them.
- The next time someone angers me, I'm going to ask myself, "Will *angering* (striking out, hitting back, acting spiteful) really help me get what I want right now?" Just stopping a few seconds to think, will likely cause me to want to change my behavior to a more positive one so I can be a winner over myself and the problem.

Figure 4.6. My Personal Plan for Self-Control: My Psychological Car

My plan

Here are the good habits I know I have:

1. _____

2. _____

3. _____

Here are three behaviors I am now working on and hope to have achieved three weeks (21 days) from today:

1. _____

2. _____

3. _____

I will check my progress on (date)_____

My plan for checking my progress will be

1. Day by day _____

2. Week by week _____

3. Other _____

Thought for this day: "Angering is a useless habit. Unless I *choose* to control myself, someone will be forced to control me. The choice is mine!"

My personal plan above was negotiated with my teacher and was reviewed co-operatively on (date)_____

_____ (student signature)

_____(teacher signature)

Figure 4.6. Continued

SOURCE: Full acknowledgment and publishing credit given to *The TEPSA Journal* (Fall 1992), No. 46: 24-27 and 34, for an earlier treatise by coauthor Bradley on the same subject.

Remember: it is a negotiated plan but it also contains some of the good habits a student already knows he has, the principles he wishes to implement, and the time-line he is going to follow in seeing that these habits are acquired.

We want our students to look at the world as a miraculous place, rather than a place in which to be full of anger. A personalized self-discipline plan will become a cognitive map once the plan's behavior patterns become imprinted on the student's thinking. We are helping youths have the feeling that they do have some control over their own destiny, rather than being reminded through school rules that they are unable to think in meaningful ways. Children are further down the road of being good citizens in society when they are enabled to see the importance of looking inside themselves for motivation and moral behavior.

Setting Goals That Matter

Traditionally, when students have been asked to set goals, most turned out to be academic, designed to please the teacher. Such goals would include "I want to read 100 books to get a reading circle award this year"; "I want to move to an *A* in geography by the end of the semester"; "My short-term goal is to make 100 in spelling each week, but my long-term goal is to be a better composition writer, spelling the words I use correctly." These are worthy goals. You will find, however, that self-directed learners discover the reality that comes from setting goals.

In the past, teachers helped students set academic goals to work on. But many goals fell by the wayside if the teacher did not keep prodding. Even then, only about 2% of the students were able to write down their goals for living. But for today's self-directed learners, the goal is so important that it acts like a magnet, drawing the goal setter toward it. The teacher thus spends more time helping students decide what goals are worth giving time to. So teachers and students spend time together discussing the students' needs, because goals arise from needs. Students are taught to become more responsible for understanding their needs and setting reasonable goals to achieve them.

Consider the following guidelines for self-directed learners seeking to define appropriate goals. Students should select the approach that they think will work best for them. If it does not fit, they simply select another one and move ahead.

Student Questions

1. Ask yourself the age-old questions of growing up: "What do I want to be when I get older? What will it take to get

there? What pitfalls might I suffer? What skills must I have? How will I likely change personally? What do I have to offer right now? What is my first step toward this new goal?"

2. Review the benefits you would receive if someone employed you. What do you not have that some employer might expect you to demonstrate? Patience? Good work habits? Specific knowledge? Creative talents? People skills? Computer knowledge? Necessary work skills?

3. Think about how much responsibility you are taking for your life right now. Do others have to tell you what to do, or do you behave on your own? Do your work and on time? Take care of your health? Get to places on time? Study at school without being told? Do something extra on your assignments, or just do enough to get by?

4. Do you give more time to looking at what your friends are choosing for their goals, or are you doing what you think you ought to do for yourself?

Specific Suggestions for Goal Setting

1. Write down goals that will give meaning to your life. Have some "fun" goals, some new study goals, some new academic goals, and some new goals for working with people.

(Goals will depend on individual preference, but students will still come to the teacher for direction. The greatest help of the teacher here is to seek congruency between lifestyle and goals. This is a major awakening for some students. For example, one student may set a goal to improve his people skills, but forget to practice these skills on a daily basis on his peers. This should be called to his attention.)

2. Make your goals powerful, but be sure they are concrete, compact, and specific. Avoid loosely stated goals ("I want to be a better person"), and turn them into something you can really do ("I want to say positive things to people every

day so I will become well liked and they will want to be around me.")

3. Check to see that your goals are measurable. When will you feel you have accomplished at least some part of achieving your goal? How much will you have to do before you will be pleased with your accomplishment? Will a dozen ways of helping you work with people be enough? If you have chosen to work on anger, when will you know you have arrived at your goal? Set your limits and set them soon. After a little bit of work on your chosen goals, set time limits—at what date do you expect to have achieved your goals?

4. For your first attempt at goal setting, try setting just three goals. If you set five or six, it may be too much and take too much time. You are apt to fail if you try to work on too many goals.

5. Talk with your teacher to be certain your goals are within your level of understanding and power to make happen. Write the goals that focus on your own behavior and the knowledge that you can change. To reach your chosen goals, that is exactly what you will have to do—change!

6. Brainstorm, read all you can on your goal, talk to experts about it, and don't be afraid to dream. Look back 2 or 3 years and identify your most successful experiences. Think about your past failures too. How might this reflection guide your goal setting? Past mistakes help us set future goals.

Reinforcing Goals Through Mental Imagery

Visualize your chosen goal as if it were already met. Close your eyes and look back over your goals and try to identify some essential steps you took to achieve one. The mind keeps coming up with new ways of exploring and achieving your goal. Your mind is a powerful computer—always working! Seeing the goal in your mind and thinking about it as already met strengthens the belief that it will come about. Seeing your goal as already met, what are people saying to you now? What do they think about you? What do these "remarks" make you think about yourself? What are you doing now that you were not able to do before? How do you feel about yourself now?

If you get a feel of what people will say early in the process, it will help you to keep striving to meet your goal. Your mind wants to hear kind remarks from others. However, don't just work for what others will say. Work for how you will feel about yourself—that's much more important than what others will say.

Look back at the steps you visualized using to reach your goal. What was the first step? Now decide to take action on that first step when you open your eyes. Add more details for reaching this first step. Then praise yourself for this accomplishment. Sometimes it may be necessary to stop your mental imaging, look at your steps again, and balance your thoughts so that you still visualize reaching your chosen goal.

You are taking yourself beyond merely thinking about your goals. You are also learning that through your mind's eye, you can achieve your predictions. You will discover the processes through which you bring them about, and that these processes can be used again and again.

So You Want to Be a Self-Directed Learner? Here's How!

(The following outline can be used as a strategy for starting students on their own plan of goal attainment. Although some of it can be used as a dialogue between student and teacher, most of it should be presented to the whole group, so all can listen, exchange ideas, and learn from each other's comments.)

1. Stop following others blindly, and start leading yourself with vision. Picture yourself as being in control of self, and with just a little effort, you will become what you have envisioned as your goal. Don't just try to manage your life. That's not enough to make it big in life. Managing your school life may seem a narrow experience, but *leading* yourself in school is a "biggie"—if you can't lead yourself, how can you expect to lead others?

2. How do you lead yourself? Set acceptable, worthy, and achievable goals. Then decide how you are going to influence yourself to reach them. A goal could be short-term ("I want to have my paper written by tomorrow morning"), or long-term ("By the end of the month, I want to have completed all of my notebook on the Civil War").

3. Kick procrastination out of your vocabulary and life today. Don't put off what you need to be doing today. Get it done! Then feel good about yourself after you do it. Make yourself do what you should today and after a short time, you will acquire the habit of doing it on time! Reward yourself from time to time for taking the extra effort, perhaps with an hour's visit after school with a friend.

4. Set realistic goals for yourself, and enjoy getting there. Listening to what the teacher says can be an asset to your planning; working joyfully toward your goal can be an invigorating experience. If your goals are important to you, you will enjoy working on them all the more. Choose projects that will help you grow—out of each may come new ideas to explore. What are two or three goals that are realistic to you and your needs? Are you capable of making 10 shots out of 10 at the free-throw line in basketball? If not, maybe you can make 5 out of 10 this week, 6 out of 10 two weeks from now, and 8 of 10 in a couple of months. Keep a daily record of your goals and misses; try to do better each day, then after a few weeks, check the record of your shooting. When you plan to do better, most of the time you will do better.

Suppose you wish to write a book on dogs for an assignment in English class, to show how well you can use grammar rules for composition. Your short-range goal is to write a page a day so at the end of the 6-week period, you will have something to show your teacher. Your long-range goal results in a booklet 30 pages long (6 weeks × 5 school days a week = 30 days—and pages). With clever planning, and no procrastination, you have made a hard job easier than you thought possible.

Try to negotiate some assignments with your teacher where you can follow her wishes, but choose your own way of getting there. Be smart! Don't wait until the end of 6 weeks to show her some of your work. In just a few moments, she can tell you if you are on the right track.

5. Plan how you intend to accomplish your goal, then write it down and file it for future reference. Without a written plan, it is difficult to determine what to do if something goes wrong. Consider the following points in devising your plan. Do you intend to write your daily page at home or school? Will you write at the same time each day? If you miss a day, when will you make it up?

With respect to your basketball, could your brother, father, or close friend judge your shots some afternoon and keep passing the ball back to you from under the basket? Would a videotape made by Dad help you know more about how you're shooting? How about comparing these tapes with some future tapes to see your progress?

6. Know what stands between you and your goals. A self-directed learner asks, "Why haven't I already achieved the goal I set out to do?" The answers may be simple, but important: It's a new goal; I tried it once and failed; it's a school goal and I had little to do with it; and so on. But these are goals you have chosen for yourself; they're the ones you *want* to do. If you can list the obstacles, you can usually write down a solution, sometimes with help from your teacher, parents, or other experts. One obstacle is often your own mistake—failing to set a target date for completing the goal.

7. Explore your thoughts regarding the following ideas:

> Some people set goals very low, so they can achieve them with little effort.
> How should you balance time between work, family, fun, television?
> List five or six things every night that you want to accomplish the next day, so your mind can think about them all night while you sleep.

Should you break long-term goals into doable tasks, like putting a puzzle together a piece at a time?

Is it better to work a little each day toward your chosen goals, or take a day off and work all day on a single goal?

Of the five or six temporary goals you listed above, why not prioritize them?

How long is your attention span? 10 minutes? 15? 30? An hour? You should consider how long you can enthusiastically work on your goals. Just as it's better to study a little each day in preparation for a test, it is important to work within your attention span a few minutes each day toward achieving a goal.

For a minute a day, stop and look at your goals (Figure 4.7), then see if your behavior matches your goals.

SDL starts when the learner becomes aware of some need for learning. It may be to acquire certain information for an assignment, or a more personal need of acquiring or improving a certain skill. It could be the desire to develop greater self-confidence or competence in performing a role. It may merely be to satisfy a curiosity about an idea—to simply enjoy the pleasure of learning. One fourth-grade student, who wanted to improve his class presentations, was encouraged to follow these steps:

1. List the behaviors required of a good speaker.
2. Check the behaviors you want, or the ones you wish to improve.
3. Assess your present level of performance.
4. Identify the gaps between your ideal model and your present performance.
5. Watch a videotape and see how a speaker models the competencies you have listed.
6. Remember: Performance assessment in the area of skills requires that you do the action and have your proficiency rated.

As a self-directed learner, how to arrive at your goals				
START with				
	Goals I want	Possible roadblocks	Solutions to roadblocks	Progress to date
1.				
2.				
3.				
4.				
5.				

Target dates to finish goals

Goal 1 _____

Goal 2. _____

Goal 3. _____

Goal 4. _____

Goal 5. _____

How I intend to keep refining goals accomplished

_____

_____

_____

_____

_____

Figure 4.7. A Plan to Make Changes in My Goals

7. Make a rating scale that will show the competencies of a good speaker and how you might measure your strengths and weaknesses in each.

8. Try your rating scale on two or three speakers in another class.

9. Have someone videotape or record your performance, and rate you.

10. Evaluate your own performance by looking at the rating sheets of your presentation.

11. Practice your weak points, refine your strong behaviors.

12. Reassess in a few days on another performance. Compare your rating scales again. Review both tapes. Ask for teacher input if you have not already received it.

Just preparing a rating scale is a great learning experience for a student (Figure 4.8). It is difficult to practice competencies unless one knows what they are. This student also learned how to transpose the average of his ratings onto a single rating-scale sheet so he ended up with a profile showing his strengths and weaknesses. An additional thrill came when others asked to use his rating scale. He was also pleased when he checked his competencies on his new rating scale with three experienced speakers: the local mayor, a university professor, and the building principal.

Goals take on a new meaning in the self-directed learner's life. School direction and involvement may be apparent in them, but the goals are of the student's making. They affect him or her not only at the moment, but also in the future. In the past, schools set the goals for children before they ever arrived in the classroom, but today youngsters set their own goals when they arrive at school. From that point forward, they secure school help in reaching those goals in the most effective manner possible. Self-directed learners especially need this assistance, because their goals become established standards to guide their whole lives, changing, modifying, and acquiring new goals as they seem necessary. Goals should be high priorities in life. Effective goal setting is outcome-based education used at its highest level. Figure 4.9 lists goal-setting criteria designed to be memorized in youth and used into adulthood.

Things to watch	Ratings									
	1 Low	2	3	4	5	6	7	8	9	10 High
Quality of opening remarks										
Accurate facts										
Quality of illustrations										
Use of gestures in delivery										
Logical sequence of development										
Appropriateness of humor to make a point										
Evident sincerity										
Pronunciation of words										
Pacing/speed of delivery										
Eye contact with audience										
Body movements on floor (position/stature)										
Securing audience attention (interesting)										
Voice projection										

Figure 4.8. A Model of the Most Important Behaviors of a Public Speaker

NOTE: This rating scale was prepared by a fifth-grade student in the Lane (1992) study.

Criteria: The goal should be ... (Follow with a personal description of the chosen goal.)

1. *Meaningful*: I want to improve how I work effectively with people. People who make it big in the world know how to work with others.

2. *Measurable:* I will identify three areas in which I need to improve my working habits (how I act, what I say, following through). I will concentrate 5 minutes a day on developing the powers that will help produce what I have chosen to become through personal effort and practice.

3. *Manageable*: I will be able to find this time each day because I will be helping myself do better the things that should be done anyway. My initial thrust, however, will be to learn and refine how I deal with others—I can immediately try an idea on someone and get their response to it. Second, I can get help on this from my teachers (along with my other assignments), as well as from other experts and friends who can give advice on a daily basis.

4. *Maneuvering and Motivating*: One can't create new goals without also creating a need for new decisions to be made. New decisions, however, when they're genuine and relevant, are invigorating and uplifting. They motivate! They challenge! They give one an inner drive that just won't quit.

5. *Magnificent*: Even with goals, a person tends to drift—if the goals are selected by others or are perceived as being of minimal level. Poor goals are distracting, unrewarding— and usually useless. Goals should be deemed worthy (by yourself and others), respectable, and rich with the promise that the structure and measures to achieve them ensure that they will be fulfilled at the highest level. Magnificent goals are always the result of empowerment and quality control. They don't just "pop up" accidentally—they are conceived in the mind, incubated in the spirit, dreamed about, and designed to produce the greatest possible influence on your life. Magnificent goals empower you, help you avoid or remove forces that may block their attainment. Magnificent goals provide hope for tomorrow, faith in yourself, and most of all, *enthusiasm for the next sunrise!*

Figure 4.9. Criteria for Goal Setting

5 Looking at a Self-Directed-Learning Classroom

Changing Perceptions About Learning

Teachers are always busy, no matter what type of teaching style they use. But if students are learning through their own projects and activities, the teacher may have time to schedule individual help. Just because youngsters are encouraged to choose some new paths does not mean teachers should throw away group techniques that have worked well in the past. For instance, each day the teacher might give several 5-minute lectures on certain skills, and students can sign up for the one they feel best suits their needs.

For example, if they are expected to write a piece of poetry but lack the necessary skills, they can sign up for "poetry skills." So a teacher may have 6 to 12 students out of a class of 24 receiving instruction. Why teach poetry skills to just one student if you can offer it to six, eight, or more?

The great mistake of today's educational system is the fact that children are increasingly judged not by their human qualities, but by their academic accomplishments—both are needed. We respect academic power, but we hope to see an international assessment that compares how well our students turn out as people, using interpersonal skills not just for a job, but for lifelong living and learning, and a commitment to making a better society.

Self-Directed Learners Need Time

We are always hurrying children. "If you don't hurry, you'll miss your bus!" "Your papers were due 3 minutes ago. I'll have to take your paper now!" Self-directed students need time to let ideas incubate; they need time to try them, to revise them. Ideas that really stick in the adult mind are the ones that have been thought about deeply, that have been tried and tested and can be recalled automatically when needed.

Self-directing classrooms should have a slower pace so children have time to think. We sometimes teach like the world was on fire and kids' papers are needed to keep the fire burning. We should not let the rapid pace of our lives interfere with meaningful teacher-student relationships.

Schools should design a curriculum that would assist young people in examining their basic perceptions about society and how it can be improved. Four questions are basic to such a curriculum:

▓ What kind of society now exists and what are its dominant trends?

▓ What kind of society is likely to emerge in the near future (say, the year 2000) if these trends continue?

▓ What kind of society is preferable, given your perceptions of essential values?

▓ If the society predicted is different from the one preferred, what can the individual—alone or as part of a group—do toward eliminating the discrepancy between them? (Van Til, 1974, pp. 270-271)

These questions are particularly relevant to teachers who wish to help young people formulate perceptions that get them to think more deeply. Young people need to study, on one hand, youth's rejection of adult culture and, on the other, to remember that most utopias are inadequate or irrelevant. There would be disaster if youths rejected everything for which a democratic society stands. The guideline questions can also apply to personal development and students' self-analysis. They can assess their perceptions by asking: What kind of person am I now? What will I become if my present habits persist? What kind of person would I like to become? What can I do now about tendencies and preferences that conflict? The new curriculum must take into account a student's personal goals and how they are reached.

The "School of Perception"

A school based on perception—and the accompanying SDL techniques—focuses on common outcomes. Its success does not depend on the whims of individual teachers but on how well each teacher understands the common goal and uses instruction to bring it about. The classroom unit is not the most efficient or effective instructional component. What really counts is the concerted opinions of the teachers about what the school should do and their own relationships to that goal.

In the school of perception, teachers are hired to increase the thinking powers of children. The method of school organization (multiage grouping, team teaching, nongradedness, self-contained classrooms) does not ensure that thinking is taking place. When the staff understands the goal and works toward it as a group, school organization takes on real meaning.

Self-Directed Learning and At-Risk Students

What can SDL do for at-risk students? Students at risk in one area are likely to be at risk in other areas as well (Frymier, 1992). SDL can build up their self-concept and give them success in one area that they can carry over to another. If students are not reading, help them write something they can read; review these skills. Then follow up with the same type of activity in social studies. Give them a list of simple social studies words to learn, instead of a generalized spelling list with no words they immediately need. Later, have them write a paragraph in science. Using the same reading skills and writing principles, they will learn. Their hurting will lessen, and their confidence and skills will become stronger.

Growing up is risky business, but children who learn how to reach out on their own to solve their problems will survive better. Some at-risk students seem to have the capability to save themselves once they find a simple plan that they can adhere to—they no longer see their situation as hopeless. Evidently, with enough self-generated excitement about school through the aid of SDL, and with time and training, most inwardly perceived learning limits and anxieties disappear. Students who can train themselves out of feeling that they are "not as good as the competition" have done something for themselves that is not far short of a miracle.

Student Empowerment—Less Control
Brings More Control

In a self-directing classroom, the daily curriculum includes more opportunities for students to empower themselves, instead of being controlled totally by teachers. Adult-imposed discipline gives children no reason to develop self-discipline. As long as adults are around they will behave, but without that external control, some situations collapse into sheer chaos—"The teacher's out of the room, so let's go crazy!" These are the sentiments of children who grow up having discipline forced on them. If students did not learn earlier that discipline is based on an internal code of ethics, something to internalize and use to be effective, intelligent, and self-fulfilling, they usually perceive discipline of any kind as something to be avoided, because they associate the word with punishment.

We must help children adopt an internal code of ethics to which they can refer for guidance. When you help a child acquire perceptions that tell her why she ought to be responsible for her own control, and that it has nothing to do with being caught or doing what you believe, but is something she must internalize, then you assist her with perceptions that will govern her actions in personal, constructive ways when you are not around (see Figure 5.1).

Ethics is taking responsibility for your own actions—treating others as you wish to be treated, holding to a standard of conduct that does not change just because a situation changes. It is the business of school to assist children in determining and implementing their own livable codes of ethics. Moreover, once they find a personal code, teachers must help them develop solid commitment to it. It takes strong, solid commitment to stick to a chosen plan. Teachers need to explain the principles in the codes to make sure they are congruent with the behaviors they should elicit in practice. It is still up to students to develop their own self-discipline in everything they do. But don't just talk about a code of ethics; affirm the principles and values that make them up. Live the codes yourself. Model them. If we don't, who will?

Gallup polls in recent years indicate that more than 80% of American parents want public schools to teach moral values. We ought to oblige—and involve the parents. We don't deny the importance of continuing to teach "the basics." Reading, writing, and arithmetic are still important subjects—but it is time to add a fourth and fifth R: respect and responsibility (Lickona, 1988).

A wise teacher can channel the energy of young people into living for what is right. We house the next generation of parents, statesmen, and citizens. We believe that it is the moral responsibility of each teacher to help children focus on what it takes to make a better world. We should immerse our students in understandings as simple as the following guidelines for developing a personal code of ethics:

- Earn your neighbor's love and respect.
- Model the behaviors you would like to see in others.
- Treat others as you wish to be treated yourself.
- When you take something for nothing, you degrade yourself.
- When you give your word, you have a moral obligation to follow through.
- Defend people who are right as quickly as you tend to pounce on someone who is wrong.

All students could benefit from discussions that focus on their perceptual powers; they need to hear and analyze information that will affect their perceptions. We need to ask students:

1. *What motivates you to learn what you believe you should?* If teachers help children discover through stories, videos, and personal admonitions that "knowledge is power," most students will want to become powerful learners. But they have to hear every day from their teachers how they are becoming powerful thinkers. Although no teacher can make a student learn, a good teacher sets things up so a student *wants* to learn.

2. *What needs do you have right now that you wish to satisfy?* Explain to children that how they behave at the moment depends on the perceptions they hold about proper behavior. For example, whether they behave well or badly in the classroom to get what they want are choices—their choices. Students need to understand that by making a better choice, they open up avenues for demonstrating better behavior. He can always try a new, better behavior to get what he wants—all he has to do is try. When second and third graders grasp the meaning of being responsible for every behavior, they can actually control for "better behavior," and by the time they enter the middle grades, will be more in charge of their own lives.

3. *How strong are you when your friends try to pressure you to do what they want?* Are you psychologically strong enough to combat the wrong types of peer pressure? Each student should understand, "A person's actions come from his thoughts; if I can control my thinking, I can control my actions." The student who has been taught to be strong psychologically, to believe in himself, who believes that what he does is through his own choice, will be unwilling to let others pressure him into using drugs, or to go along with the crowd on anything that lowers his feelings of self-esteem.

Figure 5.1. Enhancing Students' Perceptual Powers

- Don't just "work" for someone—work as if you own the business.
- Don't distort the truth—seek to deliver the exact facts as you understand them.

Self-Directed Learning
Affects the Principal's Territory

Restructuring for SDL brings some revealing and delightful changes to the principal's major areas of responsibility. But what happens in the classroom affects the total school environment. As teachers are trained for SDL responsibilities, you will see gradual but consistent changes.

Classroom posters, daily mottoes, and catchy incentive statements on chalkboards will change.

The atmosphere in the school office will change. If you have been handling control problems, try saying in a faculty meeting, "I've been handling the students you send me for discipline. I will continue to do this to assist you. But from now on, for each student you send me each day to be disciplined, that same day send me two good students. Let's look for the 'good apples' in our school and send them to me." This alone will change your whole school's attitude toward the office (see Figure 5.2).

The lunchroom will become a quieter, more pleasant place for eating and socializing. Because teachers are aiding children to get in charge of their lives everywhere in school, many will concentrate on the lunchroom. During the first 30 days of this new procedure, students who don't behave in the lunchroom are returned to the classroom to be supervised by a designated authority—perhaps a volunteer parent, or a classroom teacher. This should be a secluded area, with little student traffic and no movement or conversation allowed. Teachers will begin to resolve problems, and so will the students, before they ever have to come to you. During this 30-day period, walk through the lunchroom, using a soft voice, shaking hands with some children for doing such a good job, and encouraging them.

Teachers' lesson planning will change. Because students will have options in their assignments, there will often be times when no students will be doing the same thing in the same way or perhaps even at the same time. If students are studying the solar system, for example, one may use a filmstrip to demonstrate his report, whereas another may have collected pictures of the solar system to show his ideas to others. The first goal may remain the

Figure 5.2. The Principal's Office

same, but each student may arrives at it by different routes. The teacher will involve students in designing some lessons, because in the design lie creative ways of implementing it. So even at the starting point, they will find several options for doing assignments. Students will start to think about what plan they will use to learn what is to be taught; they will have to self-direct—have their plan approved by the teacher before they can start to implement the assignment.

A new mood will be evident among teachers and students in their conversations and behaviors. For example, a great self-directing kindergarten teacher posted statements like these in conspicuous spots throughout the classroom. They urge children to become responsible for their lessons, lives, and actions:

- It takes courage to take a risk.
- It is intelligent to ask for help.
- We are free to make mistakes here—we learn from those.
- Use quiet voices while you work.
- We never hurt anyone—on the inside or the outside.
- Listen while others are talking.

■ Be seen being in charge of yourself at all times.

■ Help someone today—without their having to ask.

■ Don't call anyone a name you don't want to be called.

■ See the good in someone today—tell them you like what they did.

■ Be a model yourself—someone is watching you.

In classrooms, you will hear,

> Jimmy, I'm so proud of how you arranged the materials for your group's self-directing projects; you not only had them ready but knew who was to do what.

> For 2 whole months I've not had one child have to come to this room to eat—how nice it is to know you can go out to a restaurant and not embarrass yourself or your parents.

> I can't let you demonstrate that type of behavior; let's sit down right now and work out a better plan! Then you can take it down to the principal's office and let her approve it. She likes to see all new plans.

Aren't those statements better than these?

> Do you want to go the principal's office?

> You're a real troublemaker—I've had it with you.

> Don't talk. We've got work to do!

> Can't you do anything without my help?

To put it all into perspective—when students start to understand what self-initiation, -propulsion, -motivation, -control, -monitoring, -evaluation, -consideration, -discipline, and -love truly mean, then anger, hopelessness, and helplessness just seem to disappear gradually. William James (1890) put it beautifully: "An individual has many selves; the self he really believes he is, the self he realistically aspires to be, the ideal self, the self he hopes to be, the self he thinks others see, the self he fears he might be now."

Volunteer work with parents and guardians will take a new twist. There is too much wasted talent in local communities. Many potential volunteers hold degrees, have fabulous skills, and will double their efforts and zeal when they are asked to work on uplifting projects for their own children and others'. Parents readily get into the mood of helping when dull routines (mimeographing, monitoring, cleaning, correcting papers, shuttle service) give way to a higher level of use for their valuable time. Imagine scenarios like these:

I'm here today to take my third-grade daughter Mary to five areas in town to get pictures for her "big little book" on what our town does to beautify itself.

As a family, we've chosen to put a greenery display in the corner of the lunchroom for Joe's self-directing project. Thanks for the space!

Checking in to let you know we've brought the small farm animals in and they're in the long trailer for the kids to begin taking pictures and videos for the librarian. Our three fifth-grade neighborhood kids are in charge of this project, and they're all excited about preparing an animal unit for the primary kids.

An Interesting Question

Howard Hill was probably the greatest archer of all time, or so the story goes. He was so accurate that he killed an elephant, a couple of Bengal tigers, and an African lion with a bow and arrow. He could shoot one arrow and hit the bull's-eye dead center, then split the first arrow with a second shot.

What if I suggest a contest between Howard Hill and a very good fifth-grade archer? But I want to impose a handicap on Hill for the contest. I want him blindfolded—then I'll know my student can outshoot him.

Now you're probably thinking, "Who couldn't? So could I! The analogy is ridiculous. How can any person, including Howard Hill, hit a target he can't see?"

That's a good question. Here's another: "If my student can't hit a target he can't see, how can he ever hit a goal he doesn't have?"

Unless we set goals with children—precise, clearly set goals— they will not realize the maximum potential that lies within them. But when a student is self-directing and sets some real goals for life, he can home in accurately on a target.

There are all kinds of worthy goals, goals worth setting, goals that will make a difference in people's lives. How about urging children to leave the world a little better than it was when they first entered it? For example, how about prompting them to assist a person or organization that needs help? How about teaching kids to set their standards high enough so that the skills they learn will keep them out of poverty? Why not teach kids that they should acquire at least seven *saleable* skills before they finish school?

Remember—before you try to help children set goals, first help them with their roles—identifying the contributions to society they might make, the natural talents they have and the skills they must learn, the characteristics it takes to be a good public servant or business owner. When students target roles, they will set their own goals. And when someone sees their goals clearly, life becomes more joyous. Once you find out who you are, you give off joy in almost anything you choose to do.

6 Self-Directed Learning in the Classroom

The Teacher's Territory

In the following chapter, Todd Hoffman, a fourth-grade teacher in the Armstrong Elementary School in Dallas, shows how a teacher can use SDL and how the principal's influence can be felt inside the classroom as well as outside it.

As a fourth-grade teacher, I have found that creating self-directed, self-regulated learners produces powerful results. But the first step in creating a class of self-directed learners is to instill a sense of safety, not only physically but also mentally, socially, and emotionally. This safe environment must be achieved before any real self-motivated learning takes place. Social and emotional support is low when a behavior, action, or comment—by teacher or student—stifles participation or willingness to express a viewpoint. Genuine praise or compliments by the teacher do not always bring positive results. The learning process is at its peak

95

when we have high expectations for all students (taking into account ability levels so we don't cause frustration).

Take Time for Change

I spend many hours at the beginning of a new school year creating a positive, safe environment in the classroom. Many times if a conflict evolves among the students, I ask them to put away their assignments, and we simply talk. I allow them to discuss their concerns and conflicts. It amazes many students that I would take this much time, because they have been taught that learning can take place only when the teacher is talking. It is important to let the children guide the conversation and be involved in this process. This shows them that they play a role, that they are important and affect their surroundings. If this philosophy carries through the school years, we will help to mold students who see themselves as individuals who can make decisions and be responsible for their actions. Moreover, they will learn that they have some control over their destiny.

Start With "Teaming"

Often, high expectations bring about risk taking and do not always allow children to work out problems as a team. So early in the year, we instill the team spirit. "We" replaces "I" in the classroom, and the team (or family) concept generates a feeling of community. We usually talk about our "team" instead of "class," and we are "teammates," not "classmates." Most children can identify with the sports theme. The idea that we are stronger as a group than as 20 to 25 individuals is a perfect way to bring about a less threatening classroom environment.

The results of the team approach are encouraging. It shows children on a small scale that they matter—they can make someone feel good or bad, can help or not help a teammate. They have decision-making powers and there are consequences for their actions. I tell them, "When you self-direct, you have people appreciate your actions and help you in return. Or you turn others off and let the team down."

A good example of self-directing behavior was a student who got into trouble in the lunchroom for inappropriate behavior. When I approached, he was crying. He said, "I let the team down." Not, "It was someone else's fault," or "My parents will be upset!" I didn't even have to give the typical "teacher talk." I simply let him guide his own thinking and see the relationship between his actions and the results. I know he gained more self-awareness from the episode than what I could have "lectured into him."

Set Goals, Not Rules

The word *rule* connotes no thinking, no choice, no individual way to do something. I don't use the word rule in my classroom. We set goals! Personal goal setting tells children that they have a responsibility to set standards they should achieve. It teaches moral conduct and self-regulation, and children see positive goals as the right thing to do. They think, "I don't have to arrive at these goals at all costs, but it feels good to reach them."

Along the way, the children find their own way to reach a goal—the way that best works for them. This teaches them that they control their own destinies, and they begin setting their own goals with greater confidence and consistency.

Provide Options and Creative Choices

It is important to emphasize the word *choice*. Children need to be aware that they do have choices and it is up to them to make responsible ones. The teacher needs to show children how their decisions affect the results. A child must see the correlation between the two to benefit from both good and bad decisions. If an adult makes an investment in the stock market, whether she has gains or losses, the smart investor wants to know why. What is the relationship between decisions and results?

The accountability and pride each student feels as a member of the team generates better behavior. If a class begins to feel pride, not just for themselves but as a unit, they see how one individual can hurt a team's reputation. So the class begins to monitor each other's behavior. This can be a tricky process and needs to be handled delicately, but if the team has been coached it becomes comfortable for the class.

Help Students Determine How They Learn Best

Once a safe environment is created, I move on to self-awareness—guiding students into getting to know how they work and learn best. Do they like to write, draw, build, talk, or use technology to get a point across? Almost all assessments for long-term projects show effective learning from individual viewpoints. What if Michelangelo had decided to paint *David* instead of sculpting him? We would still have seen the image of David and appreciated the artwork, but perhaps thought that painting was the only way to truly capture David. Thank goodness the world is not composed solely of painters but also of sculptors, builders, architects, writers, talkers, and actors. Each teacher needs to see these traits in his or her students and let the students express their knowledge with their innate, natural talents.

In our school, the principal, who promotes global learning using artifacts, time lines, and displays within the building, encourages teachers to work on real problems and issues. I do an interdisciplinary unit on rivers that includes a personalized project on the Trinity River. I ask students to show me what they have learned from reading a 15-page diary kept by a man who traveled the Trinity River in 1845. I tell them that they can choose any way to demonstrate this learning. The media specialist and I created the Rivers Project, an interdisciplinary unit based on the theme of rivers and significant water throughout the world. These basic objectives were to be met:

1. To create self-directed learners;
2. To promote cooperative learning;

3. To integrate technology; and

4. To increase students' knowledge of a major, but depleting, resource—water.

Each student was given a camera to "see" the project through his or her own eyes. Long-term projects allowed for individual learning styles to demonstrate personal learning. Students created their own slide shows. They communicated with class-rooms throughout the world about river and water pollution problems. And for evaluation, they created portfolios at the end of a 3-month-long project, so parents could view their work. The major purpose was not to score students, but to show reasons for their learning and to display their SDL styles. This decision-making process was more valuable than the diary assignment because it forced each student to stop and think, "What do I do best? What would be the best way to do this? What method do I enjoy in working with a project?"

For one artistic student, a visual learner, a mural was the best way. At 10 years old, she realized her strengths. By using her painting skill, she created a mural that depicted the man's journey in great detail. Through awareness of learning styles, not only did she master the content but translated her knowledge into some-thing to share with the class. Another group of students produced a play, writing the script, designing costumes, and making invita-tions. Because they recreated the scenario from their reading, they readily demonstrated what they learned. Another student built a model of the river bottom, complete with plant and animal life.

Although much of the interdisciplinary unit involved long-term projects, the main project was to assemble a portfolio of their experiences with rivers and water. First, we discussed what a portfolio is and what goes into one, so students went into the project agreeing on what was expected of them, which allowed a comfort level with no surprises and with fair expectations. The students discussed what would be considered as *excellence* for evaluation, came to agreement, and then set out to achieve those stipulations. Each student took pictures showing what the unit of study meant to that student—science experiments, friends in a creek, or a speaker who came to talk about pollution. Next, they put in their favorite writing assignments and other creative products.

Adults know it is easier to achieve excellence if we clearly understand what is expected. This is also true of children. Teachers are there to guide them with fair, yet challenging, expectations. The job is not to merely check how many questions a student misses, but how many answers are correct and how they were arrived at.

Learning Doesn't End With a Graded Paper

Many students come to me with the notion that they have succeeded if they make 100% on a worksheet. I don't let myself give kids exercises and drills that can be completed by everyone, assuring high grades. This gives both the teacher and students a false sense that they have learned all the necessary content. The mindless, contentless learning that takes place in schools needs to be stopped. Instead, we need to allow more open discussion, sharing of different viewpoints, and arriving at a consensus acceptable to all. As teachers, we need to show our students why they are learning new things by giving them the chance to try things in a new way. This will help them determine that learning is continuous and does not terminate when a paper is marked with a grade.

The Importance of Listening

Teachers must listen to a student's words to decipher how he thinks. The thought processes used are as important as the content learned. What street or boulevard did the student take to reach his destination? Perhaps the answer is wrong, but the journey was creative and introspective. Maybe a student's experience resulted in a different perspective being used. I am not saying that we should accept that $2 + 2 = 5$, but we need to listen to the student's thinking before we make judgment about his responses, correct or otherwise. Unless we listen, we cannot really help or, equally important, help the students help themselves.

One day, we were discussing animal adaptation and camouflage. When I asked the class if they thought the polar bear was appropriately camouflaged for its environment, all but one said yes. Most felt the polar bear could hide from its enemies better with a coat that matches its surroundings. I asked the one student why he felt differently.

He explained, "Last month, I went skiing with my family. I saw this lady who had an all-white ski outfit on. I could barely tell the difference between her and the snow. I remember thinking that I sure wouldn't wear an all-white ski outfit, because if I got lost no one would be able to find me. So, what happens if a polar bear cub gets lost from its family? It might not be found. So I think it would be better if they had a darker color for their coats."

The thought process was wonderfully replete with experiences that he translated into a persuasive argument. Even though some might consider his answer "wrong," he felt good about his answer and validated his answer with a unique and thought-provoking observation. He and the class saw the connection of how one views the world can affect one's perspective.

Keep Tuned to the Real World

I spend a great deal of time helping students see what is happening outside the classroom. I often discuss the newspaper and help them respond to what is going on. Each student must bring in a current event once a week. We discuss these articles and the TV news. For those who view the newspaper as overwhelming, I encourage watching the news on TV. This is not a reading assignment, but a global awareness assignment. We not only discuss the news events but how we might solve some of the problems. Anything that empowers students—shows them that they play a role in society—readies them for future dilemmas in the real world. This takes us back to the concept that we are responsible for our actions and have a civic duty to help one another right now, in the classroom, the school, or the neighborhood and surrounding community.

We can even become global—when we study rain forests, the students really get involved. After studying about the devastation these ecosystems face, we don't simply move on to the "desert" chapter. I harness their excitement and energy into action. We spend days discussing, brainstorming, writing letters, and campaigning for ways to preserve the rain forests. The children see how they can be a part of the solution. They want to help and to spend their energy and time because they feel like they have a voice. They see how products they use can affect the rain forest and they realize their actions have outcomes that affect us all.

The students even take their learning beyond what is discussed in class. Every year, a few students do self-directing research on the rain forest for the entire year. The worst thing for a teacher to say is, "We're done with the study of rain forests." A person, if interested, might never be "done" with a subject. As adults, we strive to become experts in a field. Why can't children also attempt to become experts? As educators, we need to teach less content and spend more time on themes that are central to living and that involve long-term projects that interest the students.

Teach Students Where to Get Information

Today, it is more important to know how to find information than it is to memorize a plethora of facts. A Chinese proverb sums up the idea: "Give a man a fish and you feed him for a day; teach a man to fish and you feed him for a lifetime."

If we give a child a fact, she will probably remember that fact for a few days, but what happens 5 years down the road? She won't retain it unless she draws a value from it. We need to teach children to find the facts that will keep them "fed" for a lifetime.

Have Students Demonstrate
What They Have Learned

Avoid excessive paper-and-pencil tests as the only evaluation procedure. We need to give students a chance to demonstrate learning in their own ways. Of course, it is important to model excellence and have students demonstrate mastery. But if we make all decisions for students, both moral and educational, all we will have is a group of dependent and unsure individuals who are unable to make confident decisions for themselves.

Some of the more powerful ways to teach are not through telling youths what to think, but in giving them examples from which they can draw their own conclusions and encouraging them to search for truth through self-discovery and self-directing research shared with others. Students have not truly learned until they have shared their findings with others. Through sharing and dialogue, they learn more and so do their listeners.

Principals Also Teach

My principal is always looking for ways to encourage students to learn within the classroom, but he also emphasizes use of knowledge outside the classroom. For example, the principal grooms parents to run the lunchroom program, to assist us in teaching children, and to participate with us and advise us in instilling a new curricular program.

Additionally, he has developed interesting SDL centers in the school so students are challenged outside of typical classroom lessons. For instance, an artist who has children in our school painted a time line on the lunchroom walls, and as teachers we are challenged to answer students' questions about it. Pictures by great artists, sculptures, and poems are placed around the school, thus encouraging teachers to develop lessons that include these works. A "Texas Room," housing large wall maps, pictures, and outstanding reference material, sparks our enthusiasm to help youngsters develop self-directing projects so they can learn more on their own. Our computer room is designed to serve students in doing their projects; the computers are not just to learn on—they are to serve the students anytime they need to use them. This access helps students to get the feel of using equipment as adults do at work every day. Most students feel that once they have learned how to run a piece of equipment, the learning task is finished. It is amazing how many cannot see how using the machine makes their work easier. It is at the point of knowing how to run the machines that a lot of our best teaching begins. We teach students how to *use* that skill to enhance subsequent learning assignments.

Most principals have been taught that their major job is to go into classrooms, evaluate teachers' instruction, and see firsthand if students are acquiring relevant content. Our principal goes beyond classroom territory and has a goal of making the total school a learning experience for both teachers and students. If we are effective in the classroom, students have self-directing skills that they can employ in doing the higher level of learning that he has provided in various areas—library, playground, lunchroom, hallways, assemblies, and music, PE, and art classes. It is not by chance that our students are more self-directing than students in schools elsewhere. None of our students, parents, teachers, or principal leave attaining SDL skills to chance—we collaboratively work toward preset goals. Most are not only met successfully but usually go beyond minimum standards because our students are eager to demonstrate quality performance. A number of parents also provide remarkable service—money, labor, encouragement, and moral support. They know that the more self-directing their children become, the more ready they will be to meet the demands of the future.

Todd Hoffman

What Does a Self-Directing
Teacher Look Like?

You, and educators such as Todd Hoffman, are promoting SDL
skills, but the *lecture method* is still used predominantly in classrooms across the country. How do you change these teachers over
to self-directing methods and skills? Lectures are fine, but 180
days of them is too much (even for college professors). In a 10- to
15-minute lecture, there are many creative ways to involve and
engage students in self-directing acts. The teacher might supply
information along with the usual visual and auditory aids
(filmstrips, videocassettes, films, and the like), then ask students
to raise questions, talk over the information, and then
demonstrate ways of using that information in a problem, project,
or paper. Traditional teaching works for about half of our students,
so it can't be all bad. But good, productive teachers use more
approaches than simply lecturing. Teachers who extend their
self-directing skills into teaching will have a lot to carry over into
any lecture methods they use.

Briefly, good self-directing teachers, first, will give their students meaningful specifics, rather than generalities: "By knowing
this information____, this behavior (mental, physical, social, emo-
tional____) should be affected in this way:____." The teacher
checks for an accurate view of what is being learned, asking about
a student's daily perceptions often, instead of waiting for the
results of a written test.

Second, they will see both the academic side and the human
side of teaching as equally important. They don't simply teach
students reading, but reading *skills,* and they check the students'
point of view to see how reading is "taking." The human side is
the most difficult side of teaching. When you help a student learn
how to self-direct in his learning experiences, you find out about
his fears, anxieties, and hang-ups. Self-directed students take on
new incentives in reading classes. They don't read just to get a
grade or to learn the necessary skills. They learn to read because
they discover that reading *changes your life*—it not only gets you
a job but brings enjoyment too; it not only helps you, but helps you
to help others. In far too many cases, we teach reading to children

as a threat, rather than as the vehicle to increase their learning power and serve them for a lifetime. The self-directing teacher helps the learner make choices on what he reads—to make individual choices so he can gain introspection through his reading.

Third, self-directing teachers entice students to visualize answers before they respond to questions. Success happens first in the mind. Self-directed learners are taught to mentally practice their ideas over and over in their mind. Visualizing tends to help people function better in real situations. For example, a successful football coach filmed his players, but cut out the things they did wrong. He had them focus on the things they did well, their good moves. Going over what they did well, discussing these attributes, improved their overall playing. Catch people in the act of doing things right, compliment them, and they will strive to improve. They see themselves as winners and will do what it takes to get there.

Fourth, self-directing teachers encourage children to share with other students their knowledge of what and how they learn. Many people think SDL means learning alone. On the contrary, working with others allows people to practice how to deal with others, how to communicate and express themselves, how to take a stand, and how to get their point across effectively.

Fifth, they allow much of the learning pace to be determined by the learners, who select a pace best suited to their individual needs. Students become skilled at guessing how long it will take them to do an assignment and finish under the estimated time.

Sixth, they urge intermediate-grade learners to select evaluation methods that best suit their own learning preferences. In addition, learners select methods for documenting their accomplishments, so they have records of what they've learned, to refer to after they've moved on to something new. Logs, journals, diaries, notebooks, computer disks, videos, expository papers, and summary reviews can all serve these purposes. Thus, traditional weekly tests of "facts" become secondary in importance as evaluation.

Finally, self-directing teachers will show evidence of *metacognitive dialogue* between teacher and student in his or her classroom. The teacher will focus the student's attention on different ways of thinking about learning in classroom settings and everyday situations ("Why did we go on the field trip to the farm yesterday?" "Did you find out anything you didn't know before?" "How does a farm function?" "If you were in charge, what might you change about how the farmer does his work?" "How would you teach others what you now know about a farm?")

The learner will ask: "How can I remember the new things I learned about the farm?" "What new visual pictures do I have in my mind about the farm that I can write about in the future?" "What myths did I hold about farm life that I can now discard?" "If I wanted to learn more about the farm and can't visit to find out, where can I go to get more information?" Metacognitive dialogue helps students develop an awareness of their own learning. When children think, their thinking tends to focus on something in the world. But by getting children to change their perspective through metacognitive dialogue, they reflect on *how they think*.

7 Self-Directed Learning Outside the Classroom

The Principal's Territory

The following chapter is by Dr. Kenneth D. Thomas, principal of Armstrong Elementary School in Highland Park, Texas. He discusses how to empower staff, parents, and students to be more self-directing.

A major task of principals is to foster self-directing professionals, whether teachers, counselors, or librarians. A school that is self-directing is a teacher-directed school, and the principal's job is to help teachers to self-direct. If not, it is doubtful if they will model self-directing behaviors to the youngsters they teach.

Empower Teachers

For a school to be teacher directed and student centered, and ultimately more self-directing, empowerment must be shifted

108

from the principal's office and the central administration to teachers at the local campus. Leadership responsibilities will be delegated and collaborative decisions will be made by the people they affect—those involved at the campus level.

These decisions are continuous, not onetime solutions to ongoing school operations. At the moment, a key buzzword in education is "site-based decision making." Decisions concerning budget, personnel, curriculum content, and the instructional delivery system will be made at the building level. If all these decisions occur, the school is teacher directed. This shifting of power from principals and the central administration must permeate the entire district. The philosophy of top-down administration must be totally changed.

Help Children Feel Important

In the teacher-directed school, everything in the students' environment becomes a learning tool or situation. From the moment students arrive at school until they leave, the school focuses on qualitative as well as quantitative outcomes. It may be as simple as the principal greeting the children at the school entrance, setting the tone for students as well as parents— school is a friendly place where everyone is welcomed.

In our K-5 school, I greet each student by name and make positive comments as they enter the building. Parents say, "My child always wants to come through the door where you stand." The students often ask, "How do you remember everyone's name?" It's evident they feel important.

To those who ask why I take the time and effort to know each child's name, I respond, "I consider each child a client. I treat them the way I would a patient if I were a doctor, a client if I were a lawyer or real estate agent, or a member of the congregation if I were a minister. I want each child to feel important and comfortable in his or her relationship with the principal."

The title *Principal* connotes status and respect, even when it may not be earned. My goal is for the principalship to have the same status and respect as other professionals in the community—a respect that is earned and warranted.

Encourage Students

The entire learning environment of the school is one where the principal, teachers, and students are free to take risks to maximize learning. If a mistake is made, it isn't the end of the world. The teacher does not need to be reassigned or the student tested for attention deficit hyperactivity disorder. The planned risk may result in positive learning, or one may find that the project or lesson just needs to be discarded. Planned risks are much better dealt with than failure from something that was blindly attempted without any analysis. Teachers, administrators, students, and parents can build bridges of trust when things are attempted and then adopted or discarded.

Help Staff Members Become
More Self-Directing

A teacher writes,

Thanks for allowing me the experience of totally immersing myself and the students in the Rivers Project for a 12-week period. The project of studying rivers and water problems around the world went beyond my expectations regarding the research, the parental involvement, and the students' excitement. I was pleased with the open house where students shared their portfolios of accomplishments with parents and central office administrators. I plan to refine and incorporate more of the curriculum content into the project next year. Your support encouraged me to face the risk of possible failure—but we did succeed. The students are not the only ones who benefited. Knowing I wouldn't be penalized for failing, I also gained more confidence in myself.

From other teachers:

Thanks for helping me schedule all my planned activities on a calendar. Your nonjudgmental attitude helped me realize that I had really overplanned for myself and my students. You helped me to understand that the *process* of doing is more important than the *product*. With your assistance, I was able to monitor and adjust my thinking and the expectations for each person involved.

Because of your encouragement, I am getting my college work together and meeting with a professor to establish a plan for completing my doctorate. Without your prodding and letting me be flexible in leaving school early, I would have never believed this could be accomplished. You set such high standards for yourself and those around you, I am eager to live up to your expectations and accomplish this goal.

After you looked at all the committees and responsibilities I had with an especially challenging group of students, you dropped me a note, asking, "Am I expecting too much of you? Better watch, I will work a person beyond their limits." We looked at my role and decided where I could best serve the school as well as the district in some of its long-range goals. Other areas of leadership respon-sibilities were redistributed. I feel better about what I am able to accomplish and thank you for your insight.

Determine Desirable Attributes

Lead teachers in Grades K-4 said they were interested in the Math Their Way program, so we collaborated and scheduled a workshop in June. The teachers were excited about the program, and many rescheduled their vacation plans so they could be involved with this hands-on approach to teaching math.

Many of the teachers' comments can be amalgamated into: "We feel that it is not a 'you/us' environment—it is a 'we' environment." Each teacher is respected for his or her strengths. In the classroom, each person has the knowledge of the content and can use his or her unique art of teaching to help the students achieve the desired outcomes.

From these scenarios, we can determine the attributes that set apart more effective schools from the less effective. The more effective schools are those where teachers feel they have some control of decisions that affect them and support from their principal. The atmosphere in the building is conducive to learning. The entire staff feels more responsibility for student progress and outcomes, and there is a feeling that the whole school has proper emphasis placed on achievement. These attributes correspond effectively with the correlates of effective schools:

- Strong leadership
- High expectations
- Good atmosphere (orderly climate, sense of purpose, relatively quiet, pleasure in learning)
- Emphasis on reading
- Individualization
- Careful and frequent evaluation of student progress

The teacher-directed school operates under the premise that the individuals who know the most about any job are the ones who are doing it. Therefore, the supervisor's role is developing the potential of the teachers as well as the students. Teachers are responsible for the following:

- Assessing student achievement
- Determining the curriculum
- Developing that curriculum
- Selecting the materials to teach the chosen curriculum
- Planning the necessary staff development programs
- Determining the instructional style and strategies

- Scheduling
- Monitoring and evaluating programs as well as student progress

Start Self-Directed Learning When Students Arrive in the Morning

Students are allowed to enter the building whenever they arrive at school. Certain areas are designated as "teacher territory" until the official day begins, and other areas are student specific, with a minimal amount of supervision. If the gym is opened for the upper grades to play, goals are established with the help of the students. Any infractions are dealt with immediately and the consequences are administered. "Bill must not report to the gym the remainder of the week." "Sally must tell her homeroom teacher that she didn't follow her personal goals ('become more of a team member')."

The library is also open for student use. The computers are up and students know the process of checking books in and out. They can begin research, read magazines, or complete homework. Small groups may begin research on assigned topics. Teachers and students are working together in the library even before the official school day begins, and parents are also involved.

Due to our success using parent volunteers elsewhere in the school, the librarian and Library Committee recruited volunteers to assist the children in doing research in the media center. Because much of our curriculum is literature based, and social studies and science require research going beyond the textbook, we felt that if there were volunteers in the media center, teachers and students would do more research. Volunteers can be trained to help students locate materials and show them that information on various topics might be found in novels, CD-ROMs, tapes, records, and newspapers. With the assistance of the computer, research quickly goes beyond the traditional copying from the encyclopedia.

Many students do not go home immediately after school. This can either create a problem or can be made a productive time. We often have students set up areas to be used the following day. If the auditorium is to be used for a play or musical program, the students do it—with some supervision. They arrange the library for the monthly Parent-Teacher Organization (PTO) or PTA meetings, bringing in extra chairs, getting the coffee pot ready, or making a banner to welcome the parents. (My philosophy about moving anything in the building is not to pick up anything that you can get students to do.) Another task that students enjoy is delivering mail to the various rooms.

Make Every Nook and Cranny an SDL Area

At stairwell landings or other places in hallways where students wait or spend time, there is a huge picture frame, constructed so the Plexiglas can be easily removed to change the art displays. At one landing there may be a Monet, at another, a Rembrandt, or a print of a Rodin sculpture. The intent is for students to see a painting, read the artist's name, and know that it has been declared a classic. There is never a formal test about these items—just a general discussion by the teacher or a response to a student who might ask about the art.

Use Portfolios to Show Students' Journeys

Portfolios of art, music, and literature have been developed by and for teachers to enrich classroom experiences for students. These portfolios are created after a teacher has made a specific request—perhaps about art, music, or literature about the Civil War period. The librarian, music teacher, and art teacher meet with the teacher making the request and suggest items for the portfolio. The music teacher will teach songs from the portfolio, and the art teacher collects art that reflects the dress, mood, and entertainment of the era. The librarian will make a bibliography and gather materials about the Civil War in the media center. Books that tell of children's experiences during this period are put on reserve for students, or for the teacher to read to them. *Across Five Aprils* (1964) tells how the Civil War affected a family, seen from a young boy's perspective. *My Brother Sam Is Dead* (1974) tells the story of a family divided by the war. This kind of reading helps elementary students relate to the people of that period, rather than fill their minds with dates, names, and places that are quickly forgotten.

Change the Lunchroom to a Positive Learning Place

At the beginning of the year, the lunchroom monitor, assisted by the teachers, involves the students in establishing the goals of the lunchroom. Classes are given a score at the end of each lunch period for their behavior, and at the end of a week, the class with the highest score wins a soft drink party. When the children are told to line up at the end of the lunch period, the class is given their score for the day.

Specific violations are stated: "Jim went to the snack line three times. Jim, what is the goal we cooperatively established as to the number of times one can go through the snack line?" This is stated precisely and that is the end of the discussion. "Sue, do you recall that I had to remind you that you needed to sit at your table and visit with your friends there? It is not permissible to go to another table to sit when someone is coming back to his chair." By helping to establish the goals and receiving immediate feedback on behavior, the students can develop social skills. In addition, students are reminded of how the class can be affected, either positively or negatively, by the behavior of one person.

The cafeteria is also a place to display SDL ideas. In ours, historic events and individuals are illuminated on a time line mural painted around the room by one of the parents. While students are in the lunchroom, they can see what time period they are seated near and understand that history was being developed simultaneously in all parts of the world. This time line is really a simple course in humanities that students can study, ask questions about, and discuss with their teacher. Ours includes pictures running from dinosaurs through Greece and Rome, the Liberty

Bell and the Gold Rush, to Martin Luther King, Jr. and the
exploration of outer space.

Be Creative—Use All Areas for
Self-Directed Learning

The outside playground structures and solid surfaces were
painted by a group of fourth graders with the help of one father.
The students decided the younger children would enjoy a large
map of the United States painted on the concrete basketball
courts. The states were painted in various colors, but no cities or
states were labeled. This was a major debate among the fourth
graders, but they finally came to the consensus that the map
should have no names. Teachers could have maps in their rooms
so questions could be generated and the students would find the
answers when they were outside. This concept made going to the
playground a geography lesson also!

Tap Staff and Parents for SDL Projects

Another idea the teachers developed was to have parents
assist children with publishing books. The publishing center is
located in the teacher workroom and staffed with parent volunteers. Thirty volunteers attended the training sessions to learn
how to work with children in the writing and editing process. The
center's handbook includes information about the writing
process, forms to use with the student authors, and a resource file
of ideas for teachers. All teachers attended a publishing center
presentation and received the handbook. Two parents serve as
coordinators, sending out reminder notes, getting materials
ready, and recruiting other volunteers to help the children publish
their books, poems, and stories. With money from the PTO, the
center was able to have a nationally known children's author
spend a day in the school interacting with the children about
writing.

Make Partners of Parents

And don't forget guardians, grandparents, and graduates! Each has something to offer your school. One factor that separates an outstanding school from an excellent school is the involvement of parents. All parents are advocates for their children, no matter what their economic status. They are the main factor that can cause teaching to be rewarding or discouraging. One of the National Educational Goals for the year 2000 is that schools will "promote partnerships that will increase parental involvement and participation" (*America 2000,* 1991). Parents in our school are taught to be helpers to the teachers and advocates for their children. As parents, they receive respect and support. Parents feel free to walk into the building and interact with the teachers on a professional level or for a friendly conversation. They learn how much work and effort it takes to have an exemplary school, and they begin to ask, "What do you need?" rather than, "I don't know why that is important."

Lead, Don't Manage

By title, principals are leaders, not just managers. Leaders are interested in changing, whereas managers are more interested in maintaining; leaders in building trust, and managers in preserving the system; leaders seek to empower, managers seek to control. Leaders strive to treat people like owners ("You're doing the work so you have a say in how it's done"), whereas managers mainly deal with "renters" ("You may work here, but you don't own any of it or have much say in how things are done"). School staff will not self-direct efficiently unless they have a role in determining how things should be done in their area of jurisdiction. Therefore, I trust teachers to make their schedules, to negotiate with me when differences occur, and if we differ on an issue, to convince me they are right. I am willing to change and I trust them to be "owners" of schedules, special programs, parental communication, and so on. When people under your charge know you trust them to make good decisions, they make better decisions and do more!

Let Your Teachers Own the Schedules

Teachers at each grade level are scheduled to have common planning periods during the school day. Because of this scheduling, they are required to meet once a week as a group and plan the activities for their grade level. They coordinate field trips, order grade-specific materials, and plan their curriculum for the month. One teacher is designated grade-level chairperson, who meets with other grade-level chairs and the principal once a month. At this meeting, they determine particular curriculum issues and needs for each grade level.

The grade-level chair also presents to the Campus Leadership Council items to be discussed, such as a plan for students going from one location to another in the building. The council developed the guidelines, and the implementation of the plan was by and with the teachers. It was not an administrative decision given to the teachers to enforce. Yes, had the principal made the initial decision it would have been quicker, but the teachers would have had no ownership of the goals and students would have been automatically sent to the office for any deviation. Because the teachers formulated the goals, they handled the infractions. So although time may be saved initially, implementation and regulation of goals should remain with the teachers.

Talented Students Need
Self-Directing Skills Too

Parents are usually eager to have you assist their youngsters and will demonstrate their willingness to help in any way they can. But if they don't, it is up to the principal to convince them of this need while the child is willing, eager, and easy to teach. But not all children, even those with hidden talents, are "turned on" learners. Some lack social skills, are cranky, don't study, seem listless, won't participate, have poor grades, and are in trouble most of the time. Yet they, too, deserve their place in the sun, and if you don't capture them now, the nation loses their best contributions.

Once these students are identified, there are generally enough adult professionals around to assist these young learners. With a little phone calling and creativity, you can identify experts who would be willing to assist if they are just asked to do so. Your school should not only serve as the catalyst but reserve its right to guide any assistance, whether it has been volunteered, drafted, or secured on a contractual basis.

Each year, I participate with our local high school's National Honor Society (NHS). It has three major goals—scholarship, leadership, and service, but was weak on service. I asked the officers and sponsor if they would be willing to work with some of the children that we turned up in our search for talent who might need special help before we could discover their hidden talents. They were eager to help.

The NHS secondary students can decide with whom they would like to work, and they volunteer to work 1 hour a week for the whole year with their student. The NHS students were encouraged to interact with their charges—take them on walks, bike rides, trips to museums, anything that would create a lot of dialogue and mutual friendship. Two-hour movies were to be avoided—anything that limited talking was discouraged. No money could be spent on the young student, other than an occasional ice cream cone or soda.

One girl, the valedictorian of her graduating class, worked with a second-grade girl whom we believed to be academically talented, but who was hard to teach, had no social skills, wouldn't study, and didn't seem to care much about life. After a short time, the second grader asked her buddy, "How did you get to be a valedictorian?" The older girl said, "Well, I have to study, and study harder than all others. It isn't easy, but I make myself do it. I can see you're smart too. If you'd use some of my techniques you could be a valedictorian like me." The second grader had grown to admire her, and said, "That's what I'm going to do—I'm going to become a valedictorian." She began to concentrate on building strong social skills, watched her remarks in class, read more, took pride in her appearance, and began to study. Now she's in third grade and making all As.

One NHS student, the high school quarterback, gave his time to a student who had high sports interest but who lacked confidence, some skills, and a willingness to work hard. He did not always match preliminary training with what it takes to be a sports star. In a few weeks the quarterback had created such a change in this young student that the child and his parents were attending the high school football games. The "buddy-study" program really made a tremendous change in the behavior of this child.

I worked with a 10-year-old boy who really stood out in our computer classes. One day after school, I asked where he was going in such a hurry. When he said he had to get to his uncle's television shop to work, I said, "Let me go with you!" He showed me a computer he had built himself and some of the things he had fixed. Of course, his uncle couldn't hire him because of his age, but he let the kid work (with the parents' approval) an hour after school in his shop. This talented young boy was instrumental in setting up the computer laboratory for a large local university. We are careful not to exploit him, but he keeps our computers in order and practically teaches some of the classes for his peers. They rely on him and so do we. This is another talented student that society needs.

One of our teachers enters all the children in poetry contests, but gives special attention to talented poets. One of this country's greatest wasted natural resources is the hidden talent of our students. The intriguing thing about talented youngsters is that once they learn what it takes to move forward in improving their ability, they self-direct and joyfully forge ahead. Rarely do they complain of the extra effort it takes, the extra hours they must put in, or the odd hours they must train to excel. Moreover, once they get on a satisfying program, they often want to help others on their own and to return something to the school for getting them on the right track. In my opinion, SDL principles are worth their salt even if they were used only to bring out the best in talented and gifted youngsters.

But if talented students need SDL skills, the less talented children profit all the more, because SDL techniques allow them to work at their highest levels of performance. It seems immoral to ask kids to do assigned school work while neglecting their own capabilities. Self-directing schools can remedy this error!

What part of a school is really the principal's territory? Organizing for student success, so students see their own ideas in action! Organizing for success of each teacher! Organizing for high-quality input by parents! And organizing so that local businesses, institutions, and organizations can be tapped for the best they have to offer the school. If the principal is self-directing, both teachers and students can also be more self-directing.

Kenneth D. Thomas

 **8**

Becoming a
Self-Directing School

So, as a principal, you want to change your school? Then you must exercise a major principle of SDL—*first, change yourself.* Rid your mind of the "one more" syndrome—"If I had one more teacher . . . If I had a consultant on the staff who knew SDL theory . . . If I didn't have so-and-so on my faculty who never tries anything new (They've never even eaten a bagel! How can I expect them to change?)." But if you begin to see life from their standpoint, you can change them—by helping them choose to change themselves.

The following is an example encountered by coauthor Bradley:

On the way back from a meeting one night, I drove past my school and I saw two rooms with lights on. Two intermediate teachers had six to eight kids apiece in separate rooms, tutoring some for an upcoming math test, and priming the others for a "college bowl" game. It took me only a minute to see that both teachers and the kids were enjoying what they were doing. The kids were businesslike; they were involved!

I mentioned this in our faculty meeting the next morning, praising those teachers' special efforts. Two weeks later, I had another occasion to go to the school at night. I saw lights on in six rooms, including that of one of the same teachers. In addition, in one room a teacher and several parents were priming their kids for a standardized test; another room hosted six sets of parents and the teacher, trying out science experiments with materials borrowed from their homes. In yet another, fathers were reading to small groups of two or three—about 15 kids were there. It was easy to see who was enjoying it most— the fathers!

I asked the teacher why she was doing this, and she said, "I already have some mothers reading to both boys and girls during the day. With all our female teachers, I felt I had to get some males into our reading lessons so the little boys, especially, won't think reading is 'for girls only.' "

This is how to change a school—cultivate a small group who believes as you do and who will take the idea and go with it! Others may not do exactly what you would, but they will do *something* better than what they were doing. You can come up with some creative incentives to augment change in your school. It just takes a little ingenuity and a lot of personal motivation.

Another time, says Bradley,

My first PTA meeting at a junior high was a disaster! I had more staff there than parents. I called a special meeting of the executive board for the next day and told them I didn't need movie projectors, extra scissors, or more construction paper right now (although I did). I asked, "Can you come up with some 'gift certificates' for my teachers to purchase things for their room on some award basis?"

On Monday I announced to the staff, "In the next 20 days, for every parent that visits your room for an hour and then comes to our next PTA meeting, I will give you a $10 gift certificate for supplies for your room."

Some self-directing expertise immediately surfaced—three or four teachers had 9 to 10 parents visit their rooms in the next few weeks. Can you imagine the thrill of moving from 24 parents (including officers) at the first PTA meeting to a second meeting a month later with 213 parents there? The number never dropped below this figure and steadily increased to a school record of 300 parents attending—these inner-city parents learned how to offer us a lot in their school!

Self-directing experiences in your school will require a tremendous amount of trust. As a principal, you will have to be introspective and see if you are willing to place this much trust in your faculty. Explore the depth of your commitment:

1. Do you trust the capacities of your staff? If you take the risk, offer some training, and gear up your school for self-directing experiences, you will find that your own confidence, your responsibility as an administrator, and your psychological strength will multiply along with that of your staff.

2. Do you change a school by first changing teachers' attitudes about SDL effort, or do you give your teachers some examples of SDL experiences to use with children, to understand what it is all about? Most people feel that to change a habit, you must develop the attitude first, but the reverse is true—to change, one needs to practice what he wants to become, then the attitude comes. The practice brings about the habit.

Call your staff together. Brainstorm about how your school can become a self-directing enterprise. Trust them to do some of the experiences they come up with, then sit back and watch them change your school. Site-based management is based on negotiation, reward systems, individual and collective initiative. If you doubt this, talk it over with a fifth-grade teacher and get invited to the classroom. Sit and talk with students for 30 minutes about what they would do to make their class a self-directing enterprise. The students will tell you many constructive things to do, even if this is one of the better teachers in your building. This will give you new insights into the needs of children as you view the world through their eyes.

3. When teachers hear about self-directing techniques, many begin to toy with the idea without any further formalized plan initiated. The principal just has to be ready for the new things and to witness the power of some of these original thinkers, who are in every building. Some teachers with inquiring minds will band together and talk about the various activities they are using to change students to becoming more responsible learners. This group will be a catalyst for others—no one really wants to be left behind when others are receiving accolades for change.

Arrange for those who try self-directing activities to share with others. In a faculty meeting, set aside a few minutes for teachers to demonstrate what is now working in their classrooms. Give some rewards here! If a teacher presents a self-directing experience in the faculty meeting, find funds to send the teacher to a workshop and offer to be the substitute for the day. Ask the PTO to provide travel and lunch money and send some of these teachers to visit another district.

4. Do you have enough physical and mental stamina to keep encouraging teachers to change to newer techniques? What will you do if you find two or three teachers who seem psychologically incapable of change? Or will you be able to muster the strength to work with the small group in your school who, at your suggestion, simply begin to alter their stimulus-response style to take on a few self-directing experiences? Remember: The more trust and encouragement you show teachers, the more you give them responsibility for their jobs, the more deeply they accept it. But if you seek to pressure a teacher to change, to assume responsibility that he or she is unable or not willing to

assume, the attitude may become, "This is just another fad that will soon pass."

Supervision is at its best when a teacher has a chance to think through and talk about problems. Some of your best teachers feel comfortable with their present style of teaching, and they may feel threatened with a new way. Helping them overcome the fear of something new is just as important as removing the anxieties of the children they teach. All teachers will need your repeated reassurance that you expect to see mistakes, to hear some criticisms from parents, and perhaps to receive negative remarks from children who have already been conditioned.

5. What strategy should you use to advise parents and the PTO about the possibilities of SDL? Enlist the help of the PTO's executive board in developing self-directing youngsters. They can devise some meetings to inform parents. The program can be initiated on the experimental basis—if it works we keep it; if it doesn't, we go back to what we were doing in the first place. The PTO can involve parents in lunch program supervision, school activities, and clubs, so they can see firsthand how students are being taught to control their own behavior.

6. Involve middle-school youngsters in student council activities. Teach them how to use parliamentary procedure. This form of organization teaches them to take turns systematically, to respect the rights of others, and that the majority rules. See that students have ample opportunities to discuss what it takes to be in charge of one's behavior and how some students are able to do it successfully. Student modeling is important here, especially when small groups of students who work and play together can demonstrate they are in control of their actions. Offer awards for outstanding self-directive behaviors you witness.

7. When students are sent to your office for counseling, ask to see their self-discipline plans. If they don't have one, pull the form out of your file and help them write one. A good place to begin self-directing experiences is with management and control

problems. If a student already has a plan, it may need an overhaul. Offer advice and seek commitment to the changes. If the current plan is not working, negotiate a better one.

Leave no doubt in the student's mind as to the consequences if this negotiated plan is not implemented. Be gentle, but firm. It is a real learning experience for some middle school students to recognize for the first time that they are not following what they have said they were capable of doing. Most will seek to honor their own promises. Keep in mind that most adults who sign a legal paper feel a stronger commitment than if they have made only a verbal commitment. Students also feel a greater obligation when they sign a self-discipline commitment form.

You give the most help on self-directive techniques in your office as you counsel students for disruptive behaviors, or in the halls and lunchroom as you offer verbal correction. Learning to manage one's inward thoughts and emotions is just as important a part of education as learning the facts and skills of the respective disciplines, taking tests, and receiving grades. No educator should trust to luck to develop those critical attitudes that we value so highly in adult society.

Implementing Self-Directed Learning in a Site-Managed School

The concept of school-based management, with principals and teachers primarily responsible for managing school affairs, has received considerable attention. Although site-based management plans differ, SDL concepts might be adopted through on-site decision making.

SDL concepts go hand-in-hand with the philosophy of site-based management. Students learn that they are responsible for all their actions and should not blame others for their failures. In the site-based-managed school, youngsters are taught how to formulate their personal plans of self-discipline and control. The plan is in print, continuously monitored, and revised whenever needed (see Figure 8.1).

Do you need self-directing principles emphasized in your school? Carry this list of questions with you as you visit each classroom. Ask yourself, and if the timing is right, ask the teacher:

1. How often do students in this class have choices or options in their learning?

2. How often do students feel important in this classroom?

3. In this class, how many decisions that really count are students involved in making? How soon are these agreements implemented?

4. How are students responsible for their own learning in this classroom?

5. How often do these students feel in control, in charge of themselves?

6. How often is there only one right answer (written or oral) to questions asked here?

7. Do students here have personalized plans for increasing their learning power?

8. When the teacher walks into this classroom, how do the students react? Happy? Sad? Calm? Nervous? Assured? Afraid? Bored? Excited?

9. Do they often share laughter and pleasure?

10. Does the teacher mainly lecture and make assignments, or do the students and the teacher often work together?

11. Does the teacher in this classroom coach students in how to learn what she is teaching them?

12. Are the students in this class adding to their reservoir of learning strategies, or do they primarily accomplish their learning tasks by using a single, dominant learning style?

FIGURE 8.1. Questions for the Classroom

Principals who use site-based management principles encourage their staffs to assume more responsibility for academic planning. By having more opportunities to be imaginative and creative, teachers will be more open to developing the self-directing potential of their students. Principals should encourage teachers to place a reasonable amount of responsibility for learning on each child's shoulders. The quicker a student devises a plan for acquiring what teachers are offering, the sooner her academic scores and skills are bound to rise.

When the principal starts at the grassroots level, meeting with students to discuss that they are to hold themselves account-able for their own behaviors, and telling them their teachers will assist them in doing so, a new atmosphere gradually spreads within the building. Most children have not assumed respon-sibility for their own conduct at school because teachers have primarily done it for them. Although there are always a few who need supervision and help, if most students control themselves, it becomes much easier to deal with the 5% to 10% who need more help.

Being an Effective Leader

The greatest mistake a principal can make in running a school-based organization is to think he has to run a "tight ship." The inverse is true—on-site managers need to be flexible. What needs to be tightened is an understanding of teacher and student values, emotional and social constructs of the school and com-munity, and what leads people to produce results.

Good Schools Have a Process for Renewal

Most schools just drift, hoping things will get better. But if a principal focuses on the little things that make a difference, the school's whole big picture changes. SDL is a part of that big picture.

For example, assume that parental and teacher dialogue reveal that a number of students are spoiled—they do not want to work, have poor attendance, do only the minimum requirements, are not concerned about the quality of their work, and do just enough to get by. There may also be students who are model learners—they can repeat everything they have learned but seem unable to implement this knowledge in realistic form.

These students—in every school and every classroom—can be helped by SDL. They should be taught to do more than assigned lessons, because doing only the minimum is a cop-out. They need to get the job done, have materials ready for class, take pride in a job well done, and be able to demonstrate what they have learned.

Seeing that school is *satisfying* is a primary responsibility of the on-site principal, but it will take the undivided attention and involvement of teachers, students, and parents to really make it work. But on-site management, where everyone has a responsibility and is held accountable, is achievable. So is SDL. And in a large percentage of cases, SDL will not require a great increase in school expenditures. It requires only ingenuity, motivation, and positive action from everyone. It is the principal's responsibility to include all of these behaviors in the planning.

Implementing Your Planning

Do a Needs Assessment

The assumption behind the school-based management philosophy is that a modern school—one held accountable for its own progress—will consistently gather data, constantly interpret the data, and continuously adjust the curriculum, faculty expertise, student production, and executive strategies to bring about change based on the data.

In doing a needs assessment to determine if a self-directing program is needed, seek answers to the following questions. They are not all-inclusive, but are representative of what a needs assessment ought to reveal. Certainly, homework practices, doing only minimum requirements, pride in work, quality of production, behavioral change, academic achievement, and test taking could be added to the list.

1. What are the primary methods being used in our school to teach youngsters?
   __ discovery __ stimulus-response __ lecture __ discussion

2. What kind of freedom do children have to go to and from classrooms?

___ on their own ___ only if teacher accompanies them

3. Children are expected to put into action and demonstrate what they have learned:

___ all the time ___ most of the time ___ some of the time ___ rarely

4. The principal's office receives how many discipline problems?

___ many ___ several ___ a few

5. Students in our building:

___ demonstrate they are in charge of themselves ___need a lot of supervision ___ need little supervision

6. How many teachers understand the metacognitive needs of children at their grade level?

___ most ___ some ___ only a few

7. Each day each child evaluates something he or she did.

___ yes ___ no

8. Most children here know how to explore, on their own, a problem that has been assigned by their teacher.

___ yes ___ no

9. Most children know how to explore a problem that they devise for themselves.

___ yes ___ no

10. As a part of their daily teaching agenda, most teachers set out consciously to change the perceptions of children.

___ yes ___ no

11. Students here are taught to work against their own talents and skills in assessing their own performances.

___ yes ___ no

12. Teachers not only teach subject matter but give much attention to helping children remember what they are teaching them.

___ yes ___ no

Set a Time Line

Most schools get started in early August. This would be a good time to administer an assessment document to determine the extent to which, if any, SDL activities are being used in your school and to find out which teachers express an interest in exploring SDL more fully. This early assessment of *needs* will allow time to place SDL on the agenda of those groups in school districts who help with long-term planning and who, in the long run, serve as site-based management boards. These might include advisory councils, PTOs, or boards of education. Because a large number of schools still have some form of parent-teacher organization, the following time line example should be applicable to almost any group the principal wishes to assist in this new approach.

The PTO can be invited to participate immediately. The president should be encouraged to appoint a committee composed of executive board members, selected teachers, parents, and other citizens to study and analyze SDL material that you can provide them. A September meeting of this committee might well focus on how to involve parents in "teacher assistance" roles for support, once the SDL philosophy and principles are understood. Such support roles can include parents working with individual students on self-selected projects until the students can be turned loose on their own; obtaining materials and supplies for projects students will need; and helping with transportation and adult supervision.

A good principal not only leads teachers but also offers direction to PTO leaders. Early on, you can say you are willing to allow trained parents to serve along with teachers in starting SDL activities in the classrooms. You might list some special SDL activities for children that could be planned for the year and outline how teachers could involve parents. Remember, too, that senior citizens and parents with children too young for school are untapped resources who need to have timely information and increased understanding of what today's schools are about.

By November, there should be visual evidence of more parents and citizens working with teachers and students in SDL. If not, the principal should meet again with the designated committees and offer more creative ways of getting the task done. You might propose a community work project that involves SDL experiences for several students, perhaps developing a videotape for visitors to the local chamber of commerce, or a group research project, working with the local county extension agent on growing experimental seeds and doing soil tests as a part of a science class. After such projects are completed, certificates could be awarded at a short banquet for parents, children, and the volunteer assistants.

In early spring, the on-site manager should survey parents to determine how next year can be better. Remember: Parents really see schools as they were when they attended, so if you want them to go beyond those expectations, you must involve them in projects that will lift their sights. Give them some power and expect significant results! The more you give away power in site-based management, the more it comes back to you. *What you lose in power, you will gain in influence.* SDL gives new powers and responsibilities to both adults and students.

Involve People

People who are involved in selecting a program are more apt to do those things that make it work. Teachers need to have some say in what they will teach. Principals need to repeatedly ask, "Where are we going? How are we going to get there? How will we know when we've arrived?" In the past, teachers were used to policy being handed down from the central office. But now, with site-based decision making, they can be actively involved in selecting new ideas like SDL. They may volunteer to assess children in their class to determine how many self-directed learners they have already. Some may volunteer to do the planning for an SDL program for the school, if you offer some assistance. Some may offer to try the materials on an experimental basis. You will only know what they will do when you involve them and give them creative choices.

What can an on-site principal do? First, look to the staff. Identify the strengths and weaknesses of each faculty member. Who has good discipline and feels safe to turn several students loose for learning on their own? Who really tries to turn around kids who misbehave? Who gives a lot of time to the slower students? Who helps top students move beyond general assignments? These teachers can use SDL techniques.

Encourage teachers to develop each student's vision for learning. Just as adults' jobs should provide self-esteem as well as money, schools should do likewise. We need to equip children with a personal work ethic and teach them that the responsibility for learning rests on their own shoulders, not on their teacher's. Students must learn that if they can dream it, they can do it—but that no one can do it for them. The people who make it big are self-directing, not those who just do enough to get by.

Broadcast the Good News!

Seek Local Media Coverage— TV, Radio, and Newspapers

If you are the first school in the district to develop SDL concepts, local reporters who cover schools will want to know about it. Invite them in, take a few minutes to tell what the program is about, let them interview some students and teachers, and don't forget to have some supportive parents at the meeting. This coverage will not only bring support for the program but good news coverage for your school.

Write a Column for the Local Newspaper

In a brief article or two, stress that

1. Students will be demonstrating their true potential through self-directing behavior, not just acquiring knowledge, but demonstrating how to use what they've learned;

2. SDL excites youngsters to go beyond minimum standards to strive for higher levels of achievement; and

3. The program emphasizes how the mind works best, with students increasing personal thinking power by "thinking about how they think" and learning how to use those powers automatically.

Hold Some Morning Coffees

Ask the PTO executive board to select various spots that geographically cover your school community, then seek some parents in those areas who would be willing to invite 15 or 20 local people for 10:00 a.m. coffee to hear about the new SDL program. Beforehand, invite other parents to attend a seminar on SDL, then go to these coffees with handouts and information.

You should attend and conduct a few coffees yourself and ask a few teachers to do some (on released time). You may even want to take along a few students who can share their self-directing projects. This would be another good occasion to present certificates to these outstanding students, especially if their parents or relatives are there.

Inform All Parents

To be sure every parent knows what the SDL program is about, send a short description home with each child. Ask them to send back any questions they have, then compile these with your answers and send them out to all parents and teachers.

Capture Self-Directed Learning on a Video

Develop a 10-minute videotape that shows three or four episodes of students involved in SDL activities. Most schools have a parent (or even a fifth grader) who is good with a video camera. For example, show a scenario about new homework practices. Show the old way first, with a teacher announcing, "What we didn't finish today becomes your homework for tonight," and another saying, "Do pages 16 and 17 in arithmetic, review your spelling words, and do these handouts on parts of speech." Contrast these with the new homework procedures. The teacher says, "Here are two things we've learned today. Take these home tonight and devise a plan to apply these ideas in a new activity." In another episode, a teacher might say, "We've been studying contour maps. Here's an outline of a region. Take this home tonight and look at this region carefully and the legend that accompanies it. Make a prediction as to what the land and temperature is like, what might grow there, what animals might be on it and why, what occupations the people around there might have, and anything else you can tell from reading the contour lines and legend. Support your beliefs with geographical concepts and scientific facts you've learned in the past 3 days."

Appoint Standing Committees

Appoint a Student Committee

From third grade up, ask each teacher to appoint two top-notch students to be on the SDL program team. Meet with this group and outline clearly what SDL is all about. Talk about the old way of learning and the new way. Give them examples. Ask for their input. Listen to their questions and responses. Have another adult there to take notes. Ask them to return to their classes and tell their classmates what was discussed. Give them a copy of the agenda that you used as a guideline for this meeting. Put a dozen facts on it about SDL that would be helpful for them to review with their classmates. These students will become your best advocates for SDL.

Appoint a Committee for
Recognition and Celebration

This committee will determine the criteria for celebrating the achievements each student identifies as a measure of personal SDL success. An evening might be designated to show students' examples of the perceptions and skills they have acquired from the SDL program. A simple snack of hot dogs and sodas might be served to parents, teachers, and special guests. And invite the media!

For those who already have more extrinsic ways of recognizing students, reevaluate your procedures to remove superficial rewards. Have the committee determine the criteria for awarding SDL badges and certificates. Involve the art teacher and student artists. Ask them to create an SDL logo, picture, or symbol for the award. Present the awards at PTO meetings, assemblies, or other special meetings.

Appoint a Progress Committee

Have the faculty select two students, two parents, two teachers, and two PTO board members to serve on this committee, which appoints its own chairperson. (You serve as an ex officio member.) Their job is to assess the progress of the SDL program every 3 months. After each interval, a brief, written summary should be provided to each teacher.

An Example of Good Planning

The movement toward on-site management allows the principal to take more initiative in trying innovative ideas. Let us assume a principal wants to teach students how to become more self-directing. Analyzing the current environment, he discovers that the present school rules and teachers' actions have produced a *controlling* environment. He sees firsthand that students are moved from class to class, from class to lunchroom (and back), and to water fountains and restrooms under teacher supervision. His internal analysis of classroom visits reveals that most of the time teachers are telling children what to do and when to do it (also a controlling environment). An external analysis of bus drivers and parents shows they also have trouble controlling the children. A visit to the lunchroom suggests that it is a very noisy place. Some calls from parents reveal that not all children are getting home on time.

So he begins a list of the pros and cons about teaching children to assume more responsibility for their own learning and behavior. In a faculty meeting, he distributes this partial list to his teachers for review and further revision. A mission statement is firmed up and alternative ways identified of getting children to and from places they are expected to be. A few teachers declare it won't work—that you can't trust children to get to and from places on their own. But two or three of them say, "I'll do it if I can see how others do it," and 60% of the staff say they will "give it their best shot."

In answer to "How do we get there?" one teacher returning from summer school suggests a new approach to solving problems with a group. She volunteers to demonstrate the procedure in her classroom and invites others to watch. The principal volunteers to cover some classes for those who wish to view the process.

The wise principal knows it pays to set deadlines for anything you do with a group. So goals are discussed, written down, and dates set. At the beginning, he takes a video camera and films children getting to and from classes. At the end of the training, he takes pictures of how the majority of the students get to and from classes in an organized, controlled fashion without the aid of teachers. Comparing the two videotapes vividly portrays the answer to "Are we getting there?"

A next step might be adjusting for unmet goals and refining the system, including selecting students for a new student council, because they have demonstrated how well they now control their own behavior. Children take great pride in the fact that they can move around in school without supervision. Moreover, this feeling of being in charge of themselves encourages them to control their actions everywhere.

As most of the teachers become able to demonstrate self-directing experiences for children, the principal goes back to his planning model, identifies strengths and weaknesses of the non-participating teachers, offers personal help, assigns a person who has been successful to further assist them where needed, and proceeds to take the rest of his faculty members through the self-directing mission. Thus, each faculty member feels he has contributed to the experience, and goals have been reached. Even the most reticent teachers will want their students to be self-directing, once they see that other students have proven they can come and go without traditional supervision. Moreover, their students will pressure them to do so because they want the dignity of feeling grown-up.

Finally, although a principal is already empowered to make decisions about school operations, a good administrator will keep the central office apprised of what he is doing, even if, as in this case, his decision (new methods for monitoring children in hallways) requires little assistance from the central office.

Epilogue

SDL strategies turn out a new product. The student emerges from SDL experiences as a more fully functioning person. She knows her central nervous system can use data to increase thinking ability, awareness, and repertoire of knowledge. Moreover, she seems more able to trust herself in this, because she can more readily accept the consequences of her actions, correcting them if they prove less than satisfying.

Pointing out that experience of personal growth leads to a more self-fulfilled individual, Rogers (1969) wrote:

> He is able to experience all of his feelings, and is afraid of none of his feelings; he is his own sifter of evidence, but is open to evidence from all sources; he is completely engaged in the process of being and becoming himself, and thus discovers that he is soundly and realistically social; he lives completely in this moment, but learns that this is the soundest living for all time. He is a fully functioning organism, and because of the awareness of himself which flows freely in and through his experiences, he is a fully functioning person. (p. 288)

Over time, SDL develops a fuller potential within each student than do other systems of teaching and learning. SDL flourishes when students and teachers see one another, not only as mutually helpful human beings with resources to share but also as self-reliant human beings who care for themselves and for others.

There is much talk today of developing lifelong learners, starting as early as elementary school. The relationship between SDL and lifelong education is reciprocal. The early school years are the place to begin to educate youths for lifelong learning skills. SDL is simultaneously a means and an end of lifelong education, and the formal aspects of it should be gradually implemented in a child's formative years, with continuing exposure throughout the remainder of formal schooling. Self-directing education, offered in the early elementary years, provides greater assurance of continued learning throughout the adult years.

If, through this book, we have caused you to reflect on what you can do to improve the learning power of your students, to make the job of teaching easier and more inspiring for your teachers, and to attract more participation from parents, then our efforts have been worthwhile. Our nation's children will profit immeasurably.

A note of caution, however: Those who are committed to promoting SDL should be careful that in their zeal, they don't inadvertently set students up for failure. Because words like *success, achievement,* and *risk taking* are value-laden and, for some people, are less important than simply learning for enjoyment, outside intervention may raise false expectations. In other words, if success in school is measured as a high grade, a student may have the essential strategies for learning the material, but may not be able to apply the newly acquired skills in an actual composition. That student would need more help and practice applying what has been learned.

During Lane's (1992) investigation, fifth-grade students acquired a number of additional learning strategies. Witnessing the work of the experimental teachers, we found that educators must play the following roles if they are to foster SDL: modeling, coaching, mentoring, validating learning, and building confidence. Facilitating these is a threefold proposition for educators:

It requires a lot of work, considerable advance planning, and a tremendous faith in the ability of learners to take charge of their own learning. Although there is a substantial correlation between students' perceptual skills and their readiness to self-direct, the acquisition of perceptual skills and learning strategies occur independently of one another.

Some schools have done quite well in providing strategies for student learning. But what has been neglected are those experiences that involve students themselves in the perceptions essential to making meaningful connections between what they know and what they are learning. In short, students can be taught strategies to manage creatively much their own learning. Through mastery of both perceptions and learning strategies, students of the future will be empowered to become masters of the inner workings of their own minds, as well as directors of their learning experiences.

The importance of establishing self-directing schools in the United States can be seen in the predictions of futurists:

> The teacher will help students tap into educational programs customized for their particular needs. A teacher will coach students through video lectures, educational television programs, and artificial-intelligence-based programs. Only occasionally will teachers instruct classes themselves. Instead, they will be freed up to deliver the *personalized* instruction critical to educational achievement. (Hines, 1994, p. 12, italics added).

We must start preparing self-directing students now for tomorrow's needs in American education.

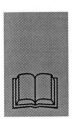

Glossary

Attribution The learner's perceptions of the causes of personal academic success or failure (Schunk, 1990b). The typical learner believes effort is the prime cause of success. Students most often attribute achievement to such causes as ability, effort, task difficulty, and luck. Whether success is judged as acceptable by the student depends on its attribution—if the student attributes some success to teacher assistance, he may believe he could not have succeeded on his own. If he then believes he has low ability, he may be unmotivated to work harder. Students must be taught to assess what behavior produced their performance, or they might not try to improve.

Cognitive Mapping A process of organizing information and concepts into pictorial representations or patterns that enhance the learning process. Cognitive maps are a way to visualize procedures or to remember facts.

Concepts Identifiable and more-or-less stable perceptions that aid in making psychological adjustments to a particular environment. Concepts are essentially the higher mental processes of problem solving, or reasoning. Reasoning ability improves gradually with increasing perception and formation of concepts. As the learner moves vertically up the hierarchy of concepts, and horizontally to broader generalization of concepts, reasoning ability also increases, because perceptions and concepts are the principal tools for solving problems.

Control Theory The belief that nothing we do is caused by persons or situations outside ourselves (Glasser, 1986). A major emphasis is the belief that individuals have control over their thoughts, feelings, and actions. A related emphasis is the belief that people are motivated by basic needs: freedom, belonging, love, fun, power, survival, and reproduction.

Executive Processes Recognizing when a particular strategy is called for and when it is not; knowing the skills of "knowing" and how to apply them. Because using mental skills involves planning and organizing in the mind, as an executive might do, processing theorists have coined the term to describe what the student is directing his internal thoughts to do.

Metacognition (*meta* = beyond) The ability to apply systematically and articulate strategies; developing an awareness of one's own thinking; being able to create reason around the activities in which one is engaged.

Metacognitive Dialogue Focusing the learner's attention, in everyday settings, on different ways of thinking about learning; making a child's thinking an object of his own thinking ("Why do I believe as I do?").

Metacognitive Listening The process of monitoring one's understanding through the use of self-questioning.

Perception The result of interaction between sensory and central nervous system processes—sensory data interpreted within the matrix of neurological processes, motivating conditions, and other psychological variables.

Perceptual Learning Increasing the ability, through practice or experience, to extract information via the senses from the environment.

Perceptual Scale The Bradley-Lane Self-Directing Perceptual Scale (Lane, 1996) reveals a student's current perceptions on selected ideas. From it, judgments can be made for forming a personalized program of instruction.

Psychic Nutrition The satisfying feedback students give themselves for making contributions to their own lives (and others'). The best psychic nutrition comes not from outside the self but, rather, from within.

Self-Directed Learning The ability of students to take actions directed at acquiring information or skill, whether by themselves or in a group.

Self-Directed Living The ability of individuals to be in charge of their thoughts, perceptions, feelings, and actions commensurate with their maturational growth and developmental abilities.

Self-Direction The ability of individuals to take action toward acquiring information or skills and developing and maintaining positive habits of thought.

Self-Efficacy Developing and maintaining positive beliefs about learning capabilities; the power to bring about the desired result (Bandura, 1989).

Self-Regulated Learning The outcome of self-directed metacognitive, cognitive, affective, and behavioral processes and skills (McCombs & Marzano, 1990). The learning that results from behaviors that are systematically oriented toward learning goals.

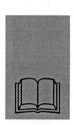

Resources

Evidence From Empirical Research
(from Lane, 1992)

Interviews of fifth-grade self-directing learners revealed the following:

1. They hold a greater confidence for learning. (They make a psychological guarantee to self: "I will learn whatever is to be learned; I can do it!")

2. Their chosen goals are more realistic and they have learned they can personally measure their accomplishment either by paper-and-pencil tests or demonstrated behavior. ("I have a way of measuring my own success or lack of it.")

3. Their own view is now more important to their teacher and to themselves. ("My own ideas can be tested against other points of view that the textbook or my teacher offers; I feel good knowing I have some good ideas I can defend and people listen.")

4. They can now fit facts and ideas they learn into old knowledge. ("I am learning how to anchor new ideas to my previous thoughts and I wasn't doing that before." One

student pointed out, "I have discovered how a southern writer differs from a northern writer as he describes the events leading up to the Civil War.")

5. They have a new understanding of the role of cooperation between the teacher and their learning. ("I'm no longer told exactly what to do, but am guided in my work by my teacher. I like the idea that I am expected to ask questions—I used to be afraid to ask; it always made me feel dumb because everybody was listening. Now everybody seeks more help and we don't laugh at each other. Often we can help each other and it isn't called cheating.")

6. They are learning things beyond "mere recall." ("Once I had an idea of what the teacher wanted me to know for a test, I stopped working on just the facts. Now, I review all ideas that are important every 2 or 3 days for a couple of minutes. I now can recall many things I learned at the first of this project, weeks ago. And it's funny, but many of those things now seem to fit together and some of my new learning seems easier. I used to think I was dumb but now I feel kind of smart. I like the new me! Believe it or not, for homework last night I took 10 minutes and listed all of the hard words from spelling lists I had taken over the past 6 weeks. I had a list of 29 words that I could spell and give the meaning of. It felt good!")

7. They obtain "psychological learning" from school as well as academic, subject matter learning. ("I hated school and blamed my teacher for what I didn't want to do. Then I discovered a neat, new idea: 'I should not blame others for my own hang-ups'—and that was exactly what I was doing. Like Ms. Lane said, 'If you practice liking school, then your attitude will change.' She's right! I did this and I'm doing real well in school now. I still don't like everything, but I don't blame my parents or teacher or principal for this. Someday I will even like science. But I like experiments, so my teacher lets me do experiments every Wednesday and Friday. I now like science on Wednesday and Friday. And my friends say, 'You must really like

science—we like the new experiments you do for us on Wednesday and Friday.' I'm reading a book I got out of the library—*101 Science Experiments.* I'm even surprising myself!")

Statements by Students Who Advocate Self-Directing Behavior (names have been changed)

(*Nancy,* sixth grade) I used to talk all the time, even during class. Now I can go to an assembly and sit with friends from other classes in the rows designated Self-Directing Students, and I don't talk at all. The students who feel they still need help with controlling themselves can choose to sit with supervising teachers until they feel safe to "go it on their own." All of us like being trusted—it causes us to put trust and faith in ourselves.

(*Joe,* fifth grade) I went to the principal's office so often, most kids thought I worked there! But my principal and I negotiated a "self-directing discipline plan" and I haven't had to go to the office for being bad for weeks. I've been back three times and reviewed how I'm doing, and he's really encouraged me. In fact, he's put me in charge of teacher supplies, and when they come in, I get to choose a friend and we take lists and distribute the materials on a little cart. I earn coupons for this—popcorn and pizza for Fridays. My behavior is a lot better. I really don't know why I acted so badly before. I guess I thought people really didn't care about me.

(*Sue,* fifth grade) I always wondered why no one trusted us to just go up and down the hall by ourselves—and why we were "shushed" all the way up and back. Gee! It feels great to walk up the hall with a friend and talk in a soft voice. None of us talk as loud as our teachers!

(*Pete,* first grade) My mother asked me why I couldn't behave at home like I was doing at school. I've stopped getting in trouble at school because I want to be in the group that can be in charge of themselves. I guess I'm going to have to do the same thing at home to keep my mother happy.

(*Les,* second grade) I read stories into a tape recorder. Then I listen to how I pronounce each word. I ask myself, "Was I clear? Did I accent the right syllable? Could others understand me? Did my words run together? Did I go too slow? Did I go too fast?" My teacher calls this self-evaluation. And I can do it. Sometimes I have to redo my work by recording it again. But I don't mind! I'm going to be a sports announcer when I grow up!

Resource B

*A Professional Development "Worthshop" on
Self-Directed Learning*

A Seven-Step Plan

1. A *worth*shop on SDL for teachers and administrators
   should focus on exploring the best answers to these questions about SDL:
   a. What do self-directed learners do that typical
      learners do not learn to do in school today?
   b. What do teachers (and administrators) who wish
      to be self-directing do that the typical teacher
      may not currently be doing?
   c. What will parents need to do for their children
      when they become immersed in self-directing
      knowledge and responsibilities? How might
      homework assignments change?
   d. What new curriculum arrangements and design
      are necessary for enhancing the SDL program?
   e. What shifts in evaluating learners will be ex-
      pected if a school becomes self-directing?
2. A portion of the worthshop should be allotted to examples
   of the new type of dialogue that will take place between
   the student and the teacher on a daily basis. These may
   be as simple as discussing the new vocabulary the teacher
   must acquire ("I see you are in charge of your life; I'm
   proud of the way you're exploring on your own!") to the
   more complex counseling dialogues ("You have identified
   that you want to eliminate the tendency you have of
   automatically saying hateful words to others. Here are
   several things we can do to help you attack this problem.")
3. Ample time should be given to the discussion of what
   constitutes a well-designed self-discipline plan. A general
   form of a student's self-discipline plan should be provided
   and discussed in detail. The group should be taken

through the various steps required to develop a strong self-discipline commitment in a student.

4. The types of perceptions that a self-directing student must acquire should be identified and discussed with the group. There should be illustrations and ideas given on how to help students make these perceptions automatic.

5. The application and use of SDL skills and perceptions in the total school environment (hallways, lunchroom, library, playground, assemblies, and the like) should be outlined and discussed. Questions related to the total environment would include, "How do we get students through the halls with limited supervision? What responsibilities does the principal have to which teachers might connect some of their own classroom experiences for developing self-directing students?"

6. Time should also be allotted for describing how signs, placards, posters, classroom bulletin boards, and other forms of visual communication will take on new wording, expression, and emphasis when self-directing concepts become a major emphasis within the school.

7. Whether the worthshop is conducted by experienced teachers who are already well versed in self-directing techniques and skills, a qualified consultant on this subject, or a team from the Consultant Center for Self-Directed Learning Programs, it would be most beneficial for each teacher to have a personal copy of the following materials:

   a. Bradley-Lane Self-Directing Perceptual Scale (Lane, 1996); and

   b. *A Personal Guide to My Own Thought Processes,* by Areglado, Bradley, and Lane (in press), a little book designed for fourth-grade students.

Resource C

Twenty Perceptions of a First Grader

Since I am in charge of my life I can . . .

1...choose to have a good day.

2...choose to cooperate with my teachers.

3...help make and cooperate with classroom rules.

4...choose to listen carefully in class.

5...talk about my feelings

6...work out ways to solve problems with other people.

7...take other people's feelings into account.

8...ask others to leave me alone.

9...get myself ready for the start of worktime at school: put toys and lunch away, get supplies and equipment, go to my seat.

10...keep my desk straight so I can find things in it.

11...choose to use my time wisely and finish my work.

12...choose to work carefully and neatly.

13...choose how to use my free time.

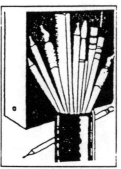

14...use materials and equipment properly and respect property.

15...talk but low enough so I don't interfere with others.

16...Go get drinks and go to the restroom on my own without having to ask to do so.

17...Walk in lines properly when asked to do so to get large groups of us where we need to go more quickly.

18...Sit with my friends in our lunchroom and quietly enjoy eating with them without disturbing others.

19...go to the library by myself
and behave properly.

20...make healthy choices about
eating, exercising, and resting.
Eat something of everything on
my school lunch tray. Drink
healthy drinks (milk, orange
juice); not just Cokes and Big
Red. Play outside or some-
where more than watch TV.

SOURCE: Cartoon panels compiled by Tom Austin, artist, Garland, Texas, and Connie Austin, teacher at Dallas ISD. Used with permission.

Resource D

Statements to Think About

The following statements may assist you in seeing what SDL can do for teachers, students, and ultimately, for society.

Read each statement and decide if SDL has something to offer your assessment of what schools ought to do to produce learners who can demonstrate greater academic productivity and wiser control of their personal lives. Every student ought to become a winner in some way. SDL can set the learner on the right path of both inward and outward control.

The principal is the most powerful change agent in a school. Such leaders must model self-directing actions themselves. Simply by asking students in hallways and daily conversations, "What are you doing to stay in charge of your own life?" and offering suggestions, you can take a giant step toward developing a self-directing school. Children believe in you. If you promote the meaning underlying the following statements, you will help children behave likewise.

The great mistake of today's educational system is the fact that children are increasingly judged, not by their human qualities but by their academic accomplishments. We respect academic power, but we hope in the future to see how well our students turn out as adults, and that they use their skills not just for job purposes but in developing qualities essential to lifelong learning and living, with an accompanying commitment to making a better society.

> You develop people like you mine gold. When you go into a gold mine you will move tons of dirt to find just one ounce of gold. But you don't go in there looking for dirt—you go in there looking for gold.
>
> —Andrew Carnegie

The worst sin towards our fellow creatures is not to hate them but to be *indifferent* to them: that's the essence of inhumanity.

—George Bernard Shaw

The best things and best people rise out of their separateness; I'm against a homogenized society because I want the cream to rise.

—Robert Frost

The object of teaching a child is to enable him to get along without a teacher.

—Elbert Hubbard

The list of ways to get involved is endless. What is important is that you begin. Someone must take the first step.

—Dennis Littky

Does Pavlov's stimulus-response theory (those drooling dogs) ring a bell? Have you ever thought about why Pavlov didn't choose a cat? Could it be that dogs are easier to deal with when you have to strap them down each day? Have you ever tried to tie a tomcat down to give him a vitamin pill, or tried to call him in when he really didn't want to come? Just like human beings, animals have different behaviors. We imagine that if Pavlov's experimental dogs had been cats instead, we would have a different philosophy about how to educate kids.

Doing everything for children—treating them as if they have no power to control themselves—weakens them and makes them feel helpless and hopeless. Limited empowerment gradually limits their zeal to be performers and producers. On the other hand, we can expect children to set goals and achieve them, to become aware of how their skills can benefit them, to feel good about themselves by giving them credit and recognition. Such rewards make them feel important and keep alive the desire to do great things. It makes them want to assume more responsibility for their existence and makes school more pleasant and self-fulfilling.

In *My Fair Lady,* Eliza says, "The difference between a lady and a flower girl is not how they behave, but how they are treated!" If we treat our students as if they are always making something of themselves, if we encourage them to self-direct, and see personal reasons to take their skills and knowledge beyond our expectations, they will do so.

References

America 2000. (1991). Washington, DC: Government Printing Office.

Areglado, R. J., Bradley, R. C., & Lane, P. S. (in press). *A personal guide to my own thought processes.*

Bandura, A. (1989). Regulation of cognitive processes through perceived self-efficacy. *Developmental Psychology, 25,* 729-735.

Biemiller, A., & Meichenbaum, D. (1992). The nature and nurture of the self-directed learner. *Educational Leadership, 50,* 75-80.

Bradley, R. C. (1991). *Teaching for "self-directed" living and learning in students—How to help students get in charge of their lives!* Denton, TX: Bassi.

Bradley, R. C. (1992). Dealing with angering behaviors in students. *TEPSA Journal, 46,* 24-27, 34.

Bradley, R. C., & Lane, P. S. (1996). *Teacher guidebook.* Manuscript in preparation.

Brock, W. E. (n.d.). *An American imperative: Higher expectations for higher education.* (Available from Wingspread Group on Higher Education, Johnson Foundation, Inc., P.O. Box 2029, Racine, WI 53404; e-mail: Internet, anonymous ftp at the University of Wisconsin-Milwaukee, ftp to csd4.csd.uwm.educ, change directory to put/wingspread/report.txt)

Brockett, R. G., & Hiemstra, R. (1991). *Self-direction in adult learning: Perspectives on theory, research, and practice*. London: Routledge.

Brown, A. L., & Smiley, S. S. (1977). Rating the importance of structural units of prose passages: A problem of meta-cognitive development. *Child Development, 48*, 1-8.

Collier, J. L. & Collier, C. (1974). *My brother Sam is dead*. New York: Four Winds Press.

Corno, L., & Rohrkemper, M. (1988). Success and failure on classroom tasks; adaptive learning and classroom tasks; adaptive learning and classroom teaching. *Elementary School Journal, 88*, 297-312.

Dunn, R. S., & Dunn, K. J. (1979). Learning styles/teaching styles. *Educational Leadership, 36*, 238-244.

Dweck, C. S., & Elliott, E. S. (1983). Achievement motivation. In P. H. Mussen (Ed.), *Handbook of child psychology*. New York: John Wiley.

Frymier, J. (1992). Children who hurt, children who fail. *Phi Delta Kappan, 74*, 257-259.

Gibson, J. J. (1951). Theories of perception. In Wayne Dennis (Ed.), *Current trends in psychological theory*. Pittsburgh: University of Pittsburgh Press.

Glasser, W. (1986). *Control theory: A new exploration of how we control our lives*. New York: Harper & Row.

Goodlad, J. I. (1983). A study of schooling: Some implications for school improvement. *Phi Delta Kappan, 64*, 552-558.

Gross, A. M., & Drabman, R. S. (1982). Teaching self-recording, self-evaluation, and self-reward to nonclinic children and adolescents. In P. Karoby & F. H. Kaner (Eds.), *Self-management and behavior change: From theory to practice* (pp. 285-315). New York: Pergamon.

Guglielmino, L. M. (1977). Development of the Self-Directed Learning Readiness Scale (Doctoral dissertation, University of Georgia, Athens, 1977). *Dissertation Abstracts International, 38*, 6467A.

Hartner, S. (1985). Processes underlying self-concept formation in children. In J. Suls & E. Greenwald (Eds.), *Psychological perspectives on the self*, vol. 3. Hillsdale, NJ: Lawrence Erlbaum.

Hines, A. (1994, January-February). Jobs and infotech, work in the information society. *The Futurist, 28,* 1.

Hunt, I. (1964). *Across five Aprils.* New York: Grosset and Dunlap.

James, W. (1890). *The principles of psychology.* New York: Henry Holt.

Knowles, M. S. (1975). *Self-directed learning: A guide for learners and teachers.* New York: Association Press.

Kohn, A. (1990). *The brighter side of human nature: Altruism and empathy in everyday life.* New York: Basic Books.

Lane, P. S. (1992). *A quasi-experimental study of 5th-graders' use of selected self-directing perceptions and learning strategies.* Unpublished doctoral dissertation, University of North Texas, Denton.

Lane, P. S. (1996). The Bradley-Lane Self-Directing Perceptual Scale. Manuscript in preparation.

Lee, H. (1960). *To kill a mockingbird.* Philadelphia: J. B. Lippincott.

Lickona, T. (1988). Educating the moral child. *Principal, 68,* 6-10.

McCombs, B. L. (1986). The role of the self-system in self-regulated learning. *Contemporary Educational Psychology, 11,* 314-332.

McCombs, B. L., & Marzano, R. J. (1990). Putting the self in self-regulated learning: The self as agent in integrating will and skill. *Educational Psychologist, 25,* 51-69.

Meyers, M., & Paris, S. G. (1987). Children's metacognitive knowledge about reading. *Journal of Educational Psychology, 70,* 680-690.

Paris, S. G., Cross, D. R., & Lipson, M. Y. (1984). Informed strategies for learning: A program to improve children's reading awareness and comprehension. *Journal of Educational Psychology, 76,* 1239-1252.

Paris, S. G., Lipson, M. Y., & Wixon, K. K. (1983). Becoming a strategic reader. *Contemporary Educational Psychology, 8,* 293-316.

Rogers, C. R. (1969). *Freedom to learn.* Columbus, OH: Charles E. Merrill.

Schunk, D. H. (1990a). *Perceptions of efficacy and classroom motivation* (TM No. 014631). Boston: American Educational Research Association. (ERIC Document Reproduction Service No. ED 317 582)

Schunk, D. H. (1990b). *Socialization and the development of self-regulated learning: The role of attributions.* Boston: American Educational Research Association. (ERIC Document Reproduction Service No. ED 317 581)

Schweinhart, L. J., Weikart, D. P., & Larner, M. B. (1986). Consequences of three preschool curriculum models through age 15. *Early Childhood Research Quarterly, 1,* 15-45.

Schweinhart, L. J., Weikart, D. P., & Larner, M. B. (1993). *Significant benefits: The High/Scope Perry Preschool study through age 27* (Monograph of the High/Scope Educational Research Foundation No. 10). Ypsilanti, MI: High/Scope Educational Research Foundation.

Skinner, E. A., Chapman, M., & Baltes, P. B. (1988). Control, means-end, and agency beliefs: A new conceptualization and its measurement during childhood. *Journal of Personality and Social Psychology, 54,* 117-133.

Van Til, W. (1974). *Curriculum: Quest for relevance.* Boston: Houghton Mifflin.

Weikart, D. P., & Schweinhart, L. J. (1993). The High/Scope curriculum for early childhood care and education. In J. L. Roopnarine & J. E. Johnson (Eds.) *Approaches to early childhood education* (pp. 195-208). New York: Merrill.

Weiking, M. (1969). A consultant role in elementary school guidance: Helping teachers increase awareness of the behavior dynamics of children. *Elementary School Guidance and Counseling, 4,* 128-135.

Zimmerman, B. J. (1990). Self-regulated learning and academic achievement: An overview. *Educational Psychologist, 25,* 3-17.

Zimmerman, B. J., & Martinez-Pons, M. (1986). Development of a structured interview for assessing student use of self-regulated learning strategies. *American Educational Research Journal, 23,* 614-628.

Zimmerman, B. J., & Martinez-Pons, M. (1988). Construct validation of a strategy model of student self-regulated learning. *Journal of Educational Psychology, 80,* 284-290.

Index